A Short History
of The Church
of Jesus Christ
of Latter-day Saints

TRUTH RESTORED

by Gordon B. Hinckley
of the Council of the Twelve Apostles
of The Church of Jesus Christ
of Latter-day Saints

D1347876

On the Cover:
Joseph Smith's First Vision

Copyright © 1979 by
Corporation of the President of
The Church of Jesus Christ
of Latter-day Saints
All Rights Reserved

The material in this book first appeared in a
larger work entitled *What of the Mormons?* (1947)
under the section "A Short History of The
Church of Jesus Christ of Latter-day Saints." The
history was later extracted and reprinted in a
separate volume entitled *Truth Restored.* The
present edition is a 1979 revision of that edition.

CONTENTS

1 Genesis 1

2 An Angel and a Book 7

3 The Power of God among Men 20

4 The Church Organized 30

5 Mormonism in Ohio 39

6 The Church in Missouri 50

7 Nauvoo, the Beautiful 60

8 The Martyrs 71

9 Exodus 81

10 To the Promised Land 93

11 Pioneering the Wilderness 104

12 Years of Conflict 115

13 Years of Endurance 129

14 The Sunshine of Good Will 138

The Prophet Joseph Smith

1 GENESIS

WESTERN New York in the early nineteenth century was essentially frontier territory, a place of opportunity to those for whom the tremendous task of clearing and breaking the virgin land held little fear. Among these were Joseph and Lucy Mack Smith and their eight children, who in 1816 came to the vicinity of Palmyra, not far from Rochester.

They were a typical New England family of English and Scottish extraction who prized the independence their fathers on both lines had fought for in the American Revolution of 1776. And they were religious folk who read the Bible and had family prayer, although like many of their kind they belonged to no church.

This condition among the people of the frontier areas of America became a matter of serious concern to religious leaders, and a crusade was begun to convert the unconverted. It was carried over a vast area from the New England states to Kentucky. In 1820 it reached western New York. The ministers of the various denominations united in their efforts, and many conversions were made among the scattered settlers. One week a Rochester paper noted: "More than 200 souls have become hopeful subjects of divine grace in Palmyra, Macedon, Manchester, Lyons and Ontario since the late revival commenced." The week following it was able to report "that in Palmyra and Macedon...more than four hundred souls have already confessed that the Lord is good."[1]

Joseph's Story

Under the impetus of this revival, four of the Smith family—the mother and three children—joined the Presbyterian Church. Joseph Jr., then fourteen years of age, also felt a strong desire to affiliate himself with a church. But he wanted to be right in so important a step, and he became deeply distressed that, although the various ministers had been united in their efforts when the revival commenced, they disagreed sharply among themselves when the converts began to file off to the various congregations. The more he listened to the conflicting arguments, the more confused he became. He reasoned that all of them could not be right, and the question as to which was recognized by God as His church greatly troubled him. In a simple, straightforward account, he tells of the course he took and of the remarkable events which followed:

"While I was laboring under the extreme difficulties caused by the contests of these parties of religionists, I was one day reading the Epistle of James, first chapter and fifth verse, which reads, *If any of you lack wisdom, let him ask of God, that giveth to all men liberally, and upbraideth not; and it shall be given him.*

"Never did any passage of scripture come with more power to the heart of man than this did at this time to mine …I reflected on it again and again, knowing that if any person needed wisdom from God, I did; for how to act I did not know, and unless I could get more wisdom than I then had, I would never know; for the teachers of religion of the different sects understood the same passages of scripture so differently as to destroy all confidence in settling the question by an appeal to the Bible.

"At length I came to the conclusion that I must either

remain in darkness and confusion, or else do as James directs, that is, ask of God. I at length came to the determination to 'ask of God,' concluding that if he gave wisdom to them that lacked wisdom, and would give liberally, and not upbraid, I might venture.

"So, in accordance with this, my determination to ask of God, I retired to the woods to make the attempt. It was on the morning of a beautiful, clear day, early in the spring of eighteen hundred and twenty. It was the first time in my life that I had made such an attempt, for amidst all my anxieties I had never as yet made the attempt to pray vocally....

"Having looked around me, and finding myself alone, I kneeled down and began to offer up the desire of my heart to God. I had scarcely done so, when immediately I was seized upon by some power which entirely overcame me, and had such an astonishing influence over me as to bind my tongue so that I could not speak. Thick darkness gathered around me, and it seemed to me for a time as if I were doomed to sudden destruction.

"But, exerting all my powers to call upon God,...and at the very moment when I was ready to sink into despair and abandon myself to destruction—not to an imaginary ruin, but to the power of some actual being from the unseen world, who had such marvelous power as I had never before felt in any being—just at this moment of great alarm, I saw a pillar of light exactly over my head, above the brightness of the sun, which descended gradually until it fell upon me.

"It no sooner appeared than I found myself delivered from the enemy which held me bound. When the light rested upon me I saw two Personages, whose brightness and glory defy all description, standing above me in the air. One of them spake unto me, calling me by name and said, pointing to the other—*This is my Beloved Son. Hear Him!*

"My object in going to inquire of the Lord was to know which of all the sects was right, that I might know which to join. No sooner, therefore, did I get possession of myself ...than I asked the Personages who stood above me in the light, which of all the sects was right—and which I should join.

"I was answered that I must join none of them,...that: 'they draw near to me with their lips, but their hearts are far from me, they teach for doctrines the commandments of men, having a form of godliness, but they deny the power thereof.' "[2]

The grove where the First Vision was received

Reactions

As might be expected, so unusual a story caused considerable excitement. In good faith he spoke of it to one of the preachers who had been engaged in the revival. The boy was taken aback when the man treated the story with contempt, telling him that such things were of the devil, that all visions and revelations had ceased with the apostles, "and that there would never be any more of them." Nor was this the end of the matter for the young boy. He soon found himself singled out for ridicule; and men, who ordinarily would have paid little attention to such a young lad, took pains to revile him. It was a source of great sorrow to him. He continues:

"It was, nevertheless, a fact that I had beheld a vision. I have thought since, that I felt much like Paul, when he made his defense before King Agrippa, and related the account of the vision he had when he saw a light and heard a voice; but still there were but few who believed him; some said he was dishonest, others said he was mad; and he was ridiculed and reviled. But all this did not destroy the reality of his vision. He had seen a vision, he knew he had, and all the persecution under heaven could not make it otherwise; and though they should persecute him unto death, yet he knew, and would know to his latest breath, that he had both seen a light and heard a voice speaking unto him, and all the world could not make him think or believe otherwise.

"So it was with me. I had actually seen a light, and in the midst of that light I saw two Personages, and they did in reality speak to me; and though I was hated and persecuted for saying that I had seen a vision, yet it was true; and while they were persecuting me, reviling me, and speaking all manner of evil against me falsely for so saying, I was led to say in my heart: Why persecute me for telling the truth? I have actually seen a vision; and who am I that I can withstand God, or why does the world think to make me deny what I have actually seen? For I had seen a vision. I knew it, and I knew that God knew it, and I could not deny it, neither dared I do it; at least I knew that by so doing I would offend God and come under condemnation."[3]

On the great problem that had perplexed him, Joseph Smith's mind was now settled. He joined none of the churches that had sought his interest. And more important, he had learned that the promise of James was true: One who lacked wisdom might ask of God, and obtain, and not be upbraided.

2

AN ANGEL
AND A BOOK

LIFE for Joseph Smith was never the same once he had told the story of his vision. For one thing, that remarkable experience had left an indelible impression upon him. The knowledge he had thus received placed him in a unique position. Nevertheless, his manner of living was not greatly different from that of the ordinary farm boy of his day, except that he was often made an object of ridicule. But he continued to work on his father's farm, to work for others in the area, and to associate with companions of his own age. Those acquainted with him describe him as a strong, active boy of cheerful disposition, who enjoyed wrestling and other sports. The story of his life and experiences at this time is again best told in his own words:

"I frequently fell into many foolish errors, and displayed the weakness of youth,...which, I am sorry to say, led me into divers temptations, offensive in the sight of God. In making this confession no one need suppose me guilty of any great or malignant sins. A disposition to commit such was never in my nature....

"In consequence of these things I often felt condemned for my weakness and imperfections; when, on the evening of [September 21, 1823], after I had retired to my bed for the night, I betook myself to prayer and supplication to Almighty God for forgiveness of all my sins and follies, and also for a manifestation to me, that I might know of my state and standing before him; for I had full confidence in obtaining a divine manifestation as I previously had done.

"While I was thus in the act of calling upon God, I discovered a light appearing in my room which continued to increase until the room was lighter than at noonday, when immediately a personage appeared at my bedside, standing in the air, for his feet did not touch the floor.

"He had on a loose robe of most exquisite whiteness. It was a whiteness beyond anything earthly I had ever seen; nor do I believe that any earthly thing could be made to appear so exceedingly white and brilliant. His hands were naked, and his arms also, a little above the wrist; so, also, were his feet naked, as were his legs, a little above the ankles. His head and neck were also bare. I could discover that he had no other clothing on but this robe, as it was open, so that I could see into his bosom.

"Not only was his robe exceedingly white, but his whole person was glorious beyond description, and his countenance truly like lightning. The room was exceedingly light, but not so very bright as immediately around his person. When I first looked upon him I was afraid; but the fear soon left me.

"He called me by name and said unto me that he was a messenger sent from the presence of God to me, and that his name was Moroni; that God had a work for me to do; and that my name should be had for good and evil among all nations, kindreds, and tongues, or that it should be both good and evil spoken of among all people."

An American Scripture

"He said there was a book deposited, written upon gold plates, giving an account of the former inhabitants of this continent, and the source from whence they sprang. He also said that the fulness of the everlasting Gospel was contained in it as delivered by the Savior to the ancient inhabitants [of America];

"Also that there were [deposited with the plates] two stones in silver bows—and these stones, fastened to a breastplate, constituted what is called the Urim and Thummim. ...The possession and use of these stones were what constituted 'seers' in ancient or former times; and...God had prepared them for the purpose of translating the book.

"After telling me these things, he commenced quoting the prophecies of the Old Testament...[Joseph then lists some of the passages of scripture quoted by Moroni.]

"Again, he told me, that when I got those plates of which he had spoken...I should not show them to any person; neither the breastplate with the Urim and Thummim; only to those to whom I should be commanded to show them; if I did I should be destroyed. While he was conversing with me about the plates, the vision was open to my mind that I could see the place where the plates were deposited, and that so clearly and distinctly that I knew the place again when I visited it.

"After this communication, I saw the light in the room begin to gather immediately around the person of him who had been speaking to me, and it continued to do so until the room was again left dark, except just around him; when, instantly I saw, as it were, a conduit open right up into heaven, and he ascended till he entirely disappeared, and the room was left as it had been before this heavenly light had made its appearance.

"I lay musing on the singularity of the scene, and marveling greatly at what had been told me by this extraordinary messenger; when, in the midst of my meditation, I suddenly discovered that my room was again beginning to get lighted, and in an instant, as it were, the same heavenly messenger was again by my bedside.

"He ... again related the very same things which he had done at his first visit, without the least variation. ... Having related these things, he again ascended as he had done before.

"By this time, so deep were the impressions made on my mind, that sleep had fled from my eyes, and I lay overwhelmed in astonishment at what I had both seen and heard. But what was my surprise when again I beheld the same messenger at my bedside, and heard him rehearse or repeat over again to me the same things as before; and added a caution...that Satan would try to tempt me (in consequence of the indigent circumstances of my father's family), to get the plates for the purpose of getting rich. This he forbade me....

"After this third visit, he again ascended into heaven as before, and I was again left to ponder on the strangeness of what I had just experienced; when almost immediately after the heavenly messenger had ascended from me the third time, the cock crowed and I found that day was approaching, so that our interviews must have occupied the whole of that night.

"I shortly after arose from my bed, and, as usual, went to the necessary labors of the day; but, in attempting to work as at other times, I found my strength so exhausted as to render me entirely unable. My father, who was laboring along with me, discovered something to be wrong with me, and told me to go home. I started with the intention of going to the house; but, in attempting to cross the fence out of the field where we were, my strength entirely failed me, and I fell helpless on the ground, and for a time was quite unconscious of anything.

"The first thing that I can recollect was a voice speaking unto me, calling me by name. I looked up, and beheld the same messenger standing over my head, surrounded by light as before. He then again related unto me all that he had related to me the previous night, and commanded me to go to my father and tell him of the vision and commandments which I had received....

"I returned to my father in the field and rehearsed the whole matter to him. He replied to me that it was of God, and told me to go and do as commanded by the messenger. I left the field, and went to the place where the messenger had told me the plates were deposited; and owing to the distinctness of the vision which I had had concerning it, I knew the place the instant that I arrived there."[1]

The Hill Cumorah

About four miles south of Palmyra is a hill of considerable size, rising abruptly on the north side and tapering to the south with a long slope. On the west side, not far from the top, as Joseph had seen it in vision, was the weathered surface of a rounded stone, the edges of which were covered with earth.

Eagerly he removed the earth so that he might get a lever under the edge. Lifting the rock, he looked into a box formed by a stone in the bottom with other stones cemented together to form the sides. There, indeed, was the treasure! —a breastplate, two stones set in silver bows, and a book of gold leaves bound together with three rings.

Anxiously he reached down to take them, but immediately felt a shock. He tried again, and received another paralyzing shock. Yet again he reached, and this time the shock was so severe as to render him weak and powerless. In his frustration he called out, "Why can I not obtain this book?"

"Because you have not kept the commandments of the

Monument to the angel Moroni on the crest of the
Hill Cumorah.

Lord," answered a voice at his side. The boy turned, and
there stood the same messenger with whom he had con-
versed during the night. Guilt overwhelmed him, and
Moroni's solemn caution flashed through the boy's mind
that Satan would try to tempt him because of the indigent
circumstances of his father's family, but that the plates of
gold were for the glory of God, and he must have no other
purpose in mind in relation to them.[2]

Thus rebuked, he was told that he would not receive
the plates at that time, but that he would undergo four
years of probation, and that during that period he should
come to the hill each year on this same day.

"Accordingly," he writes, "I went at the end of each year, and at each time I found the same messenger there, and received instructions and intelligence from him at each of our interviews, respecting what the Lord was going to do, and how and in what manner his kingdom was to be conducted in the last days....

"At length the time arrived for obtaining the plates, the Urim and Thummim, and the breastplate. On the twenty-second day of September, one thousand eight hundred and twenty-seven, having gone as usual at the end of another year to the place where they were deposited, the same heavenly messenger delivered them up to me with this charge: that I should be responsible for them; that if I should let them go carelessly, or through any neglect of mine, I should be cut off; but that if I would use all my endeavors to preserve them, until he, the messenger, should call for them, they should be protected."[3]

Troublemakers

Joseph soon learned why Moroni had charged him so strictly to guard the record taken from the hill. No sooner was it rumored that he had the plates, than efforts were made to seize them from him. To preserve them, he first carefully hid them in a hollow birch log. Then he locked them in a chest in his father's home. Later they were buried beneath the hearthstone of the family living room. A cooper's shop across the street was their next hiding place. All of these and other stratagems were employed to keep the plates safe from neighborhood mobs who raided and ransacked the Smith home and surrounding premises, and even employed a diviner in their zeal to locate the record.

On two different occasions Joseph was shot at, and it soon became apparent that he could find no peace in the neighborhood of Palmyra. Some months prior to the time he received the plates he had married Emma Hale of Harmony Township, Pennsylvania. He had met her nearly two years earlier when he boarded at her father's home while working in the vicinity for a Mr. Josiah Stoal. And when in December 1827 an invitation came from his wife's parents to live in their home at Harmony, Joseph accepted in the hope that he could find there the peace needed for the work of translation.

Once comfortably settled, he commenced work on the record. It was a strange volume, approximately six inches in width by eight inches in length, and six inches thick. The golden pages, or plates, were not quite so thick as common tin, and were bound together by three rings on one side. Approximately one-third of the plates could be turned freely, similar to the pages of a loose-leaf book, but the remaining two-thirds were "sealed" so that they could not be examined. Beautiful engravings, small and finely cut, were found on the plates.

"Reformed Egyptian" characters as they appeared on the gold plates

Joseph began his work by copying onto paper several pages of the strange characters. Some of these he translated by means of the Urim and Thummim, the "interpreters" which he had received with the plates.

Not far from Joseph's New York home lived a prosperous farmer by the name of Martin Harris. He had heard much of Joseph's experiences, and in contrast with most of the people of the community, he had shown a friendly interest in them. In February 1828, Mr. Harris called on Joseph.

"I Cannot Read a Sealed Book"

He was shown the pages of transcribed characters with some of the translations that had been made from them. They greatly interested him, and he asked permission to borrow them. Joseph consenting, he took them to New York City, and, according to his testimony, "presented the characters which had been translated, with the translation thereof, to Professor Charles Anthon, a gentleman celebrated for his literary attainments.

"Professor Anthon stated that the translation was correct, more so than any he had before seen translated from the Egyptian. I then showed him those which were not yet translated, and he said that they were Egyptian, Chaldaic, Assyriac, and Arabic; and he said they were true characters,...and that the translation of such of them as had been translated was also correct.

"I took the certificate and put it into my pocket, and was just leaving the house, when Mr. Anthon called me back, and asked me how the young man found out that there were gold plates in the place where he found them. I answered that an angel of God had revealed it unto him.

"He then said to me, 'Let me see that certificate.' I accordingly took it out of my pocket and gave it to him, when he took it and tore it to pieces, saying that there was

15

no such thing now as ministering of angels, and that if I would bring the plates to him he would translate them. I informed him that part of the plates were sealed, and that I was forbidden to bring them. He replied, 'I cannot read a sealed book.'

"I left him and went to Dr. [Samuel] Mitchell, who sanctioned what Professor Anthon had said respecting both the characters and the translation."[4]

Some years later when he was approached by an avowed detractor of Joseph Smith, Professor Anthon denied ever having commented with favor upon the characters or the translation. Yet the fact remains that Martin Harris was so impressed by the experience that he returned to Joseph Smith and then immediately proceeded to Palmyra to put his affairs in order so that he might assist with the translation.

He arrived back in Harmony on April 12, 1828. Work on the translation was begun and carried forward, although there were frequent interruptions. By June 14, 1828, Martin Harris had recorded 116 pages of manuscript from Joseph's dictation.

During this period, Mrs. Harris had asked her husband to bring the manuscript home so that she might see it. Martin asked Joseph for this privilege, but Joseph denied him.

Refusing to accept the decision, Martin continued pleading until, eventually, he was permitted to take the manuscript, provided he show it to none other than members of his immediate family. Martin agreed, but when he returned to his home he yielded to pressure from others who were curious, and evidently the work was stolen from him.

Joseph Smith realized too late that he had made a serious mistake in permitting the translation to get out of his hands. He knew that he had done wrong, and he suffered great mental anguish. This was a lesson he never forgot; nor did Martin Harris ever forget it, for he was never again permitted to assist with the translation. The lost portion was not redone, since it was evident to Joseph that his enemies could alter the original and publicly belittle him.

For the remainder of that year and the following spring he was prevented from doing any further work with the plates. Most of his time was spent in farming his own land and working for others.

Unfolding the History

On April 5, 1829, there came to his door a young man by the name of Oliver Cowdery. He was a stranger to Joseph, but he knew the Smith family, having boarded with them while teaching school in the vicinity of their home the previous season. He had heard the unusual story of the golden plates and was determined to investigate it first hand. Two days following his arrival he commenced writing as Joseph read aloud the translation of the record.

They found an unusual story. It concerned the descendants of a family who left Jerusalem about 600 B.C. The father, Lehi, had been inspired to flee the city, which was doomed to the sorrowful destruction which came shortly thereafter. Building a ship, the family crossed the ocean and landed somewhere on one of the American continents.

From this family sprang two nations known as the Nephites and the Lamanites. For the most part, the Nephites were a God-fearing people, while the Lamanites were generally indolent, quarrelsome, and wicked. The Nephites had among them the history of Israel up to the time the family had left Jerusalem, and with this they kept a record of their own nation as well as translations of writings from other civilizations they encountered.

17

Evidence that men wrote anciently on metal plates is found on these gold tablets of King Darius of Persia, which date back to 521–486 B.C.

Their history records that prophets and priests taught them principles of righteousness and administered to them the ordinances of salvation. Most remarkable of all, the Savior visited these people following his resurrection in fulfillment of his statement recorded in the Gospel of John: "Other sheep I have, which are not of this fold: them also I must bring, and they shall hear my voice, and there shall be one fold, and one shepherd."[5] He taught them the principles he had taught in Palestine and set up his church among them, giving its leadership authority identical to that which he conferred upon the Twelve Apostles in Jerusalem.

Following the teachings of Christ, these people lived in peace and happiness for generations. But as the nation grew prosperous it became wicked, despite the warnings of the prophets. Among these prophets was Mormon, who in his day kept the chronicles of the nation. From these extensive records he had compiled on plates of gold an abridged record. This he had given to his son, Moroni, who survived the destruction of the Nephite nation at the hands of the Lamanites. Moroni, prior to his death, buried the record in the Hill Cumorah, where Joseph Smith received it some fourteen centuries later. A remnant of the Lamanite nation is found today among the American Indians.

3

THE POWER OF GOD AMONG MEN

Among the doctrines taught in the ancient record was that of baptism for the remission of sins. Joseph Smith had never been baptized, for he had not become a member of any church. As he and Oliver discussed the matter, he resolved to inquire of the Lord concerning the ordinance.

They retired to the seclusion of the woods along the banks of the Susquehanna River. It was the 15th day of May 1829. While they were engaged in prayer a light appeared above them, and in it a heavenly messenger descended. He announced himself to them as John, known in scripture as John the Baptist.

The Priesthood Restored

He said he had come under the authority of Peter, James, and John, Apostles of the Lord, who held the keys of the priesthood, and that he had been sent to confer upon them the priesthood of Aaron with authority to administer in the temporal affairs of the gospel. He then laid his hands upon their heads and ordained them, saying, "Upon you my fellow servants, in the name of Messiah I confer the Priesthood of Aaron, which holds the keys of the ministering of angels, and of the gospel of repentance, and of baptism by immersion for the remission of sins."[1]

He then instructed them that with the authority of the priesthood they had received they should baptize each other by immersion. Joseph first baptized Oliver in the nearby river, and Oliver then baptized Joseph. Again men had

*Joseph Smith and Oliver Cowdery received the Aaronic
Priesthood in 1829 from the resurrected John the Baptist.*

been baptized under proper authority and in similar manner as when Jesus had gone to John in the River Jordan "to fulfill all righteousness."[2]

It was not long thereafter that another remarkable and even more significant event occurred. It took place "in the wilderness between Harmony, Susquehanna county [Pennsylvania], and Colesville, Broome county [New York], on the Susquehanna river." The ancient Apostles Peter, James, and John appeared to and conferred upon Joseph Smith and Oliver Cowdery the higher powers of the priesthood and they became "apostles and special witnesses" of Christ. With this ordination there was restored to earth the same authority to act in God's name that had been enjoyed in the primitive Church.[3]

Witnesses

In June 1829 the work of translation was completed. About three months of diligent labor had been devoted to the task, although Joseph had possessed the plates for almost two years. During all of this time he had exercised every precaution to safeguard them, lest he lose them. No one was permitted to see them.

But in the course of translation he had discovered that the record itself stated that "three witnesses shall behold it, by the power of God, besides him to whom the book shall be delivered; and they shall testify to the truth of the book and the things therein.

"And there is none other which shall view it, save it be a few according to the will of God, to bear testimony of his word unto the children of men for the Lord God hath said that the words of the faithful should speak as it were from the dead."[4]

As we have seen, among those who had materially assisted in the work were Martin Harris and Oliver Cowdery. Another young man, David Whitmer, had also been of service, though only for a brief period. When these three learned there were to be witnesses, they asked for the privilege.

Joseph inquired of the Lord and subsequently announced to the three that if they would humble themselves, theirs might be the privilege of seeing the ancient record and the responsibility of testifying to the world of what they had seen.

On a summer day in the year 1829, Joseph Smith, Oliver Cowdery, Martin Harris, and David Whitmer retired to the woods near the Whitmer home in southern New York state. In the broad light of day they knelt in prayer, Joseph praying first, followed by the others in succession. But when all had prayed, no answer was received. They repeated the procedure again without result. After this second failure, Martin Harris suggested that he withdraw from the group because he felt that it was he who stood in the way of their receiving a manifestation. With Joseph's consent, he left.

The three again knelt in prayer, and presently they beheld a light above them in the air. An angel stood before them. He held the plates in his hands and deliberately turned them leaf by leaf so that the men might see the engravings thereon. They then heard a voice above them saying, "These plates have been revealed by the power of God, and they have been translated by the power of God. The translation of them which you have seen is correct, and I command you to bear record of what you now see and hear."[5]

Joseph then left Oliver and David and went to find Martin Harris. He discovered him fervently engaged in prayer and joined him in an earnest petition to the Lord.

That petition was rewarded with an experience similar to the one had by the others.

These men wrote the following signed declaration, which appeared in the first edition of the Book of Mormon, and which has appeared in every subsequent edition:

"Be it known unto all nations, kindreds, tongues, and people, unto whom this work shall come: That we, through the grace of God the Father, and our Lord Jesus Christ, have seen the plates which contain this record, which is a record of the people of Nephi, and also of the Lamanites, their brethren, and also of the people of Jared, who came from the tower of which hath been spoken. And we also know that they have been translated by the gift and power

Oliver Cowdery   *Martin Harris*   *David Whitmer*

The three special witnesses who bore testimony of the authenticity of the Book of Mormon

of God, for his voice hath declared it unto us; wherefore we know of a surety that the work is true. And we also testify that we have seen the engravings which are upon the plates; and they have been shown unto us by the power of God, and not of man. And we declare with words of soberness, that an angel of God came down from heaven, and he brought and laid before our eyes, that we beheld and saw the plates, and the engravings thereon; and we know that it is by the grace of God, the Father, and our Lord Jesus Christ, that we beheld and bear record that these things are true. And it is marvelous in our eyes. Nevertheless, the voice of the Lord commanded us that we should bear record of it; wherefore, to be obedient unto the commandments of God, we bear testimony of these things. And we know that if we are faithful in Christ, we shall rid our garments of the blood of all men, and be found spotless before the judgment-seat of Christ, and shall dwell with him eternally in the heavens. And the honor be to the Father, and to the Son, and to the Holy Ghost, which is one God. Amen." [Signed by Oliver Cowdery, David Whitmer, and Martin Harris.]

In addition to the three witnesses, there were eight others who saw the plates. Their experience, however, was different. It happened only a day or two after the three had been shown the record by the angel.

Joseph Smith invited eight men to view the plates. They gathered about him, and he showed them the record. Again, it was in the broad light of day. Each handled the strange volume with complete liberty to leaf through the unsealed portion and closely examine the engravings. It was a simple, matter-of-fact experience in which all participated together. Their testimony on the matter follows. It also has appeared in all editions of the Book of Mormon.

"Be it known unto all nations, kindreds, tongues, and people unto whom this work shall come: That Joseph Smith, Jun., the translator of this work, has shown unto us the plates of which hath been spoken, which have the appearance of gold; and as many of the leaves as the said Smith has translated we did handle with our hands; and we also saw the engravings thereon, all of which has the appearance of ancient work, and of curious workmanship. And this we bear record with words of soberness, that the said Smith has shown unto us, for we have seen and hefted, and know of a surety that the said Smith has got the plates of which we have spoken. And we give our names unto the world, to witness unto the world that which we have seen. And we lie not, God bearing witness of it." [Signed by Christian Whitmer, Jacob Whitmer, Peter Whitmer, Jun., John Whitmer, Hiram Page, Joseph Smith Sr., Hyrum Smith, and Samuel H. Smith.]

Scores of writings deal with the statements of these two sets of witnesses. For more than a century various explanations have been offered in an attempt to account for their testimonies on some basis other than the one the witnesses declared to be the case. In the last analysis, all of the circumstances—the fact that both experiences took place in the broad light of day, that there were two widely-different types of experiences, that all concerned were mature men of demonstrated judgment—these facts, together with the future acts and declarations of these parties, all point to the conclusion that the situations in each case were just as they said they were. There was no collusion, no chicanery, no juggling. In each case it was a sober, factual experience that no participant ever forgot or denied.

All of the three witnesses left the church founded through Joseph Smith. Two of them took a strong position in opposition to him. But not one of them ever denied his testimony concerning the Book of Mormon. In fact, each, on more than one occasion up to the time of his death, reaffirmed that testimony.

Martin Harris and Oliver Cowdery returned to the Church after years of disaffection, but even when they were

The eight witnesses who bore testimony that they saw and held in their hands the gold plates from which the Book of Mormon was translated

outside the organization, they boldly declared the validity of the statement published over their names in the Book of Mormon. David Whitmer never came back into the organization, but repeatedly took the same stand as his associates had taken, and shortly before his death he published a pamphlet denying statements made in the *American Cyclopedia* and the *Encyclopaedia Britannica* to the effect that the witnesses had repudiated their testimony.

Of the eight witnesses, three left the Church, but none of them ever denied his testimony.

The Grandin Press, on which the first edition of the Book of Mormon was printed

The Book Published

With the completion of the translation, its publication was made possible through the assistance of Martin Harris, who pledged his farm to guarantee the printing costs. The work was done by Egbert B. Grandin of Palmyra, New York, who printed five thousand copies for $3,000. The volume contained more than five hundred pages and was called the Book of Mormon because the ancient prophet-leader Mormon had been its principal editor. It issued from the press in the spring of 1830.

As it was circulated and read, another type of witness to its validity appeared, perhaps more powerful than the testimony of those who had seen the plates. In the book itself are found these words: "When ye shall receive [read] these things, I would exhort you that ye would ask God, the Eternal Father, in the name of Christ, if these things are not true; and if ye shall ask with a sincere heart, with real intent, having faith in Christ, he will manifest the truth of it unto you, by the power of the Holy Ghost."[6]

The majority of the early converts came into the Church through reading the Book of Mormon. Thousands gave their lives because of their beliefs. Since its first publication, the book has been translated into more than two dozen languages, and it has affected the lives of men and women in many lands. The sufferings they have endured and the works they have accomplished are, perhaps, the strongest of all testimonies for the reality of the gold plates and their translation into the Book of Mormon—the book which has become in this generation another witness for Christ.

4

THE CHURCH ORGANIZED

NOT long after his ordination under the hands of Peter, James, and John, it was made known to Joseph Smith that the Church of Jesus Christ should again be set up in the earth. This event formally occurred the following spring in the home of Peter Whitmer in Fayette Township, Seneca County, New York.

On Tuesday, April 6, 1830, six men gathered in the Whitmer home. There were others present, but these six participated in the actual organization proceedings. Their names were Joseph Smith, Jr., Oliver Cowdery, Hyrum Smith, Peter Whitmer, Jr., Samuel H. Smith, and David Whitmer. They were all young men, their average age being twenty-four. All had been baptized previously.

The meeting was opened with "solemn prayer." After that Joseph asked those present if they were willing to accept him and Oliver Cowdery as their spiritual leaders. All agreed. Then Joseph ordained Oliver to the office of elder in the priesthood, and Oliver in turn ordained Joseph. The sacrament of the Lord's supper was administered, and then Joseph and Oliver laid their hands on the heads of the others present and confirmed them members of the Church and bestowed upon them the gift of the Holy Ghost. Next, some of the brethren were ordained to different priesthood offices.

While the meeting was in session, Joseph received a revelation in which he was designated "a seer,...a prophet, an apostle of Jesus Christ."[1] Since that time he has been referred to by the Church as "the Prophet." The Church was also instructed at this time to keep a record of all of its proceedings, a practice since carefully adhered to.

The Name of the Church

The new organization was designated by revelation as

The Church of Jesus Christ of Latter-day Saints was organized on April 6, 1830, in a log house which stood on the David Whitmer farm.

"The Church of Jesus Christ," to which the phrase "of Latter-day Saints" was later added. This is worthy of note. The Church was not named for Joseph Smith or for any other man. Nor was it named for any peculiarity of government or function, as has been the case with many religious societies. It was the Church of Jesus Christ restored to earth in "the latter day," and it was so designated.

Another matter of interest is the manner in which the officers of the Church were selected. Joseph Smith had been divinely chosen to lead the work, but his position as leader was subject to the consent of the members. Ever since that first meeting in 1830, the members of the Church have convened periodically to "sustain" or vote on those chosen to direct the affairs of the Church. No man presides without the consent of the membership.

A meeting was called for the following Sunday, and on this occasion Oliver Cowdery delivered the first public discourse in the newly founded Church. Six more individuals were baptized at the close of this meeting, and a week later seven more were added to the rolls. When the first general conference was held the following June, the membership totaled twenty-seven souls, and at the close of the conference eleven more were baptized in Seneca Lake.

In this same month, the first missionary activity was begun. Samuel H. Smith, the twenty-two-year-old brother of the Prophet, filled his knapsack with copies of the Book of Mormon and set off on a journey through neighboring towns to acquaint people with the recently published scripture. After walking twenty-five miles the first day, he approached the proprietor of an inn for a night's lodging. When the innkeeper learned of Samuel's mission, he ordered him out. The young elder slept out of doors that night.

The next day he called at the home of a Methodist minister, the Rev. John P. Greene, who was preparing to leave on a tour of his circuit. The minister was not interested in reading the book himself, but indicated that he would take the volume and keep a subscription list of any who cared to purchase a copy. Samuel returned home feeling that his efforts had been fruitless; it was unlikely that a Methodist minister would urge his flock to purchase the Book of Mormon.

But a strange thing happened. Mrs. Greene picked up the volume and became greatly interested in it. She urged her husband to read it, and both later joined the Church. This same copy fell into the hands of Brigham Young of Mendon, New York. This was his first contact with the Church. Some two years later, after careful study and investigation, he was baptized.

The book, as it was circulated by Samuel Smith and others who followed him, had a similar effect on many other future leaders of the Church. Parley P. Pratt, a Campbellite minister, chanced to read a borrowed copy and soon forsook his old ministry to join the ranks of the newly organized Church. He took the volume to his brother Orson, later renowned as a scientist and mathematician, who soon thereafter threw all of his energy into promoting the new cause. Willard Richards, a Massachusetts physician, remarked after reading one page of the volume, "God or the devil has had a hand in that book, for man never wrote it."[2] He read it through twice in ten days and joined the cause.

And so the influence of the volume increased. From it, the members of the Church received the nickname—and it is only a nickname—by which they have since been popularly known—Mormons. However, in their emphasis on this scripture of the western hemisphere, they have not diminished their advocacy of the Bible, which they regard as the word of God. These companion volumes stand hand in hand as two witnesses of the reality and divinity of the Lord Jesus Christ.

Persecution

More often than not the work was bitterly denounced in that day of religious bigotry. Shortly after the organization of the Church, Joseph Smith was arrested while conducting a meeting in Colesville, New York. He was charged with being "a disorderly person, setting the country in an uproar by preaching the Book of Mormon." The testimony introduced was as ridiculous as the charge, but no sooner was he acquitted by the judge than he was arrested on another warrant of the same nature and dragged off to another town to stand trial, again to be acquitted. Thus began the persecution that was to harass him to his death.

A Mission to the Lamanites

The second general conference of the Church was held in September, 1830. Among matters of business was the call of Oliver Cowdery to undertake a mission "into the wilderness, through the western states, and to the Indian territory." Peter Whitmer, Parley P. Pratt, and Ziba Peterson were later called to accompany him. This mission charted much of the future history of the Church.

In October the four men left their families and set out on foot. Near the city of Buffalo they met with members of the Catteraugus Indian tribe, to whom they told the story of the Book of Mormon, explaining that it contained a history of their forefathers. Many appeared interested, and the missionaries left copies of the book with those who could read.

Elder Pratt, prior to his conversion to Mormonism, had been a lay preacher of the Church of the Disciples, founded by Alexander Campbell. He was now anxious to discuss Mormonism with his former associates, and the missionaries therefore traveled to northern Ohio where lived a large group of Mr. Campbell's followers. Elder Pratt particularly sought out Sidney Rigdon, one of the leading ministers of the faith.

Mr. Rigdon cordially received the missionaries, but was skeptical of the story they told. Nevertheless, he permitted them to preach to his congregation, and he agreed to read the Book of Mormon. He was baptized shortly thereafter and became an ardent worker in the cause of Mormonism. Elder Pratt described the situation with the statement that "faith was strong, joy was great, and persecution heavy."[3]

A Harvest of Souls

Within three weeks 127 souls had been baptized. Before the missionaries left in December, a thousand members had been added to the Church.

One of the recent converts, Dr. Frederick G. Williams, accompanied the missionaries west from Ohio. They spent several days among the Wyandot Indians who lived in the western part of the state and then continued their journey to St. Louis, walking most of the way.

Of the journey west from St. Louis, Elder Pratt writes: "We travelled on foot for three hundred miles through vast prairies and through trackless wilds of snow—no beaten road; houses few and far between; and the bleak northwest wind always blowing in our faces with a keenness which would almost take the skin off the face. We travelled for whole days, from morning till night, without a house or fire, wading in snow to the knees at every step, and the cold so intense that the snow did not melt on the south side of the houses, even in the mid-day sun, for nearly six weeks. We carried on our backs our changes of clothing, several books, and corn bread and raw pork. We often ate our frozen bread and pork by the way, when the bread would be so frozen that we could not bite or penetrate any part of it but the outside crust."[4]

Arriving at Independence, Jackson County, Missouri, the elders made preparations to visit the Indians in the adjoining frontier area. They met with the chief of the Delawares, who received them kindly and listened with great interest to the story of the Book of Mormon. However, their opportunities to preach were soon limited. Government agents, at the behest of intolerant religionists, ordered the missionaries from the Indian lands. Four of them remained in Missouri for some time, while Elder Pratt returned to New York to report their labors.

The First Move Westward

When Elder Pratt reached Kirtland, Ohio, he was surprised to find Joseph Smith there, and to learn that the New York members of the Church planned to move to Ohio in the spring. Persecution in New York had increased, and the success of the missionaries in their travels had pointed the way to the future destiny of the Church in the West.

The second annual general conference was called for June 1831, in Kirtland, Ohio. By that time, most of the New York members had moved west, and the congregation present at the conference numbered two thousand. The Church had made substantial growth since the original six members met to effect the organization on April 6, 1830.

At this conference several men were ordained to the office of high priest for the first time in the Church. Also, twenty-eight elders were called to travel to western Missouri, going in pairs and preaching as they went. The Prophet pointed out that it had been revealed to him that

Joseph Smith tells a group of Indians the story of their progenitors as found in the Book of Mormon.

the Saints would there establish Zion.

These missionaries, including Joseph Smith, traveled "without purse or scrip," preaching with power as they went, constantly adding to the numbers of the Church. They arrived in Jackson County, Missouri, about the middle of July, and were followed by the entire company of Saints from Colesville, New York, who had settled temporarily in Ohio and then moved on west as a body. At a place called Kaw Township, on a portion of the present site of Kansas City, they commenced a settlement under the direction of the Prophet and Sidney Rigdon.

The first log for the first house was laid by twelve men representing the twelve tribes of Israel. The land was dedicated for the gathering of the Saints, and those present covenanted "to receive this land with thankful hearts" and pledged themselves "to keep the law of God," and to "see that others of their brethren keep the laws of God."[5]

Thus was established the first Mormon settlement in Missouri. Later in the summer, Joseph Smith, Sidney Rigdon, and other leading elders returned to Kirtland, Ohio. For the next seven years the activities of the Church were divided between these two locations a thousand miles apart —Kirtland, Ohio, near the present site of Cleveland; and Jackson County, Missouri, near the present Kansas City.

5 MORMONISM IN OHIO

THOSE years during which the activities of Mormonism were largely centered in Ohio and Missouri were among the most important and the most tragic in the history of the movement. During this time, the basic organization of Church government was established; many fundamental and distinguishing doctrines were pronounced by Joseph Smith; the work spread abroad for the first time; and, concurrent with this development, the Church was subjected to intense persecution, which cost the lives of many and from which all of the Saints suffered seriously.

While events of historical importance were going on in both locations contemporaneously, communication between the two groups was limited because of difficulties of transportation, although officers of the Church traveled from one location to the other as necessity required. For the sake of clarity, this chapter will deal with events in Ohio from 1831 to 1838, and the chapter following will treat the Missouri story for the same period.

The Holy Bible

One of the projects undertaken by Joseph Smith before his removal to Ohio was a revision of the English Bible. He did not discredit the King James' translation, but he knew, as has since been more generally recognized, that certain errors and omissions in that record had led to numerous difficulties among the sects of Christendom. He had received his first understanding of this from Moroni, who, on his initial visit in 1823, had quoted to Joseph Smith from the scripture a text altered somewhat from the language of our Bible.

Upon his arrival in Ohio, Joseph continued with this labor, working as time permitted. The changes he made indicate some interesting interpretations of parts of the scripture.

Doctrinal Standards

Inevitably, as the Church grew, various questions and problems arose. Joseph sought the Lord for guidance—and received it. Most of the revelations which have since regulated the Church were received during this Ohio-Missouri period.

These revelations deal with a great variety of subjects—the age for baptism, the organization and machinery of ecclesiastical government, the call of missionaries to special labors, counsel on diet and rules for healthful living, a prophecy on the wars that would afflict the nations, the glories of the kingdoms in the life to come, and a variety of other matters. They reflect the breadth of the gospel, and the breadth of the Prophet's thinking. Only a few can be mentioned in this brief writing.

The question as to when an individual should be baptized has been a source of endless discussion among Christian peoples. In the second or third century, the practice of baptizing infants was inaugurated and has since continued, although without scriptural warrant. In fact, one of the fundamental purposes of baptism—the remission of sins—indicates that the recipient must be capable of repentance and of leading a better life. The Book of Mormon clearly teaches against the baptism of infants as a denial of the mercy of Christ, and in November 1831, Joseph received a revelation establishing eight years as the age at which children should be baptized.

On February 16, 1832, Joseph Smith and Sidney Rigdon beheld a vision of the eternal glories. In the record of this experience they bear testimony of the reality and personality of the Savior: "And now, after the many testimonies which have been given of him, this is the testimony, last of all, which we give of him: That he lives!

"For we saw him, even on the right hand of God; and we heard the voice bearing record that he is the Only Begotten of the Father—That by him, and through him, and of him, the worlds are and were created, and the inhabitants thereof are begotten sons and daughters unto God."[1]

They then describe something of the kingdom of eternity which they saw. Men in the hereafter will not be assigned arbitrarily to heaven or hell. The Savior had said, "In my father's house are many mansions,"[2] and Paul had written of a "glory of the sun, and another glory of the moon, and another glory of the stars."[3] In the hereafter, according to the Prophet's teaching, there are various kingdoms and degrees of glory; there are various gradations of exaltation. All men will be resurrected through the atonement of Christ, but they will be graded in the life to come according to their obedience to the commandments of God.

Such teachings, flying in the face of traditional Christianity, were bound to stir the indignation of the intolerant. On the night of March 24, 1832, a mob broke into Joseph Smith's home, seized him while he slept, dragged him from the house, beat him severely, choked him into unconsciousness, and then tarred and feathered him, leaving him to die. But he regained consciousness and painfully made his way back to the house. The next day being Sunday, he preached a sermon, and among his congregation were some of the mobsters of the night before. At the conclusion of the meeting he baptized eleven people.

On the same night, Sidney Rigdon was also mobbed. He was dragged by the heels for some distance with his head bumping over the frozen ground. For days he lay in a delirium, and for a time it appeared that he would lose his life, but he eventually recovered.

A Prophecy on War

On Christmas day of this same year, 1832, Joseph Smith made a remarkable prophecy, opening with the words, "Thus saith the Lord." He prophesied that war would come upon the earth, "beginning at the rebellion of South Carolina....and the time will come that war will be poured out upon all nations." He indicated that the southern states would be divided against the northern states, and that the southern states would call upon Great Britain. The time would come when Great Britain would "call upon other nations, in order to defend themselves against [yet] other nations; and then war shall be poured out upon all nations. ...And thus, with the sword and by bloodshed the inhabitants of the earth shall mourn."[4]

Twenty-eight years later, in December 1860, South Carolina seceded from the Union. On April 12, 1861, Fort Sumpter in Charleston Bay was fired on, and the tragic Civil War began. The forces of the southern states were marshalled against those of the northern states, and the southern states in turn called upon Great Britain. Of the wars since that time, in which Britain has called upon other nations, and of the mourning and bloodshed of the inhabitants of the earth, nothing need be said in this writing. It is a matter of history known to all.

A Word of Wisdom

In February 1833, another interesting revelation was received and proclaimed to the people. It is found in section 89 of the Doctrine and Covenants and is known in Mormon literature as the Word of Wisdom. It is essentially a code of health. In it the Saints are warned against the use of tobacco, alcoholic beverages, "hot drinks," and the intemperate eating of meat. The abundant use of grains, fruits, and vegetables is advocated. A promise of "wisdom and great treasures of knowledge," together with blessings of health, is given those who obey these principles. It is an unusual document whose principles have been confirmed by modern nutritionists and medical scientists. The application of its teachings has had a salutary effect upon the physical welfare of those who have followed them.

Education

In this same period, Joseph Smith organized the "School of the Prophets." Through revelation he had been instructed that those who were to go forth to teach the glad tidings of the restoration of the gospel should first prepare themselves "by study and by faith."[5] This did not mean that those engaged in the ministry of the Church should be trained in seminaries for this purpose, choosing the vocation as one might choose the profession of doctor or lawyer. Each man holding the priesthood had the responsibility of learning enough of the work to enable him to expound and defend the doctrine.

It had been made clear by the Prophet that education was a concern of religion. Among his teachings was the principle that "the glory of God is intelligence."[6] Further, "Whatever principle of intelligence we attain unto in this life, it will rise with us in the resurrection."[7] The broad development of the mind was a rightful concern of the

Church, and for this purpose a "School of the Prophets" was established. Not only were classes in theology taught, but a renowned linguist was retained to teach Hebrew. This was a remarkable innovation in adult education on the Ohio frontier, and it was the forerunner of the extensive Mormon education system.

Church Organization Completed

At the time the Church was established, its affairs were under the direction of a presiding elder. But through revelation, other offices were added as the membership increased. Three distinct offices were established in the Aaronic Priesthood—teacher, deacon, and priest. On February 4, 1831, Edward Partridge was named "bishop unto the Church," and on January 25, 1832, Joseph Smith was sustained as President of the High Priesthood. Two counselors were later appointed to serve with him, and these three constituted what has since been known as the First Presidency of the Church.

In February 1835, a Council of Twelve Apostles was chosen, and "seventy" were called to assist the Twelve. In 1833 the father of the Prophet was ordained Patriarch to the Church, which office, the Prophet explained, corresponded to the ancient office of evangelist.

With all of these offices in the priesthood set up and filled, there was again to be found on earth the same basic organization which had existed in the primitive Church, with Apostles, seventy, elders, high priests, teachers, deacons, evangelists, and bishops.

In November 1833, Brigham Young and Heber C. Kimball, two men who were later to play an important part in the affairs of Mormonism, left their homes in Mendon, New York, and traveled to Kirtland to meet Joseph

Smith for the first time. They found the Prophet in the woods chopping and hauling wood. There began a long and devoted friendship between Joseph Smith and the man who was to succeed him as President of the Church. When that succession took place, Heber C. Kimball was to stand beside Brigham Young as his counselor in the First Presidency.

The First Temple

One of the outstanding achievements during the Kirtland period of Church history was the construction of a temple of God.

On May 4, 1833, a committee was appointed to take up a subscription for the building of the temple. It should be noted that these people had little in the way of financial resources. The leaders among them had been devoting their time and energies to missionary labors. Moreover, they had recently moved from New York to Ohio, and their means had largely been exhausted in the purchase of lands. Nevertheless, they had received what they regarded as a commandment to build a sacred house, and they set upon their task.

The question arose as to the plan and the type of materials to be used. Some thought that the building should be of frame construction or even of logs, as was generally the custom on the frontier. But Joseph told them that they were not building a house for a man, but for the Lord. "Shall we," he asked, "build a house for our God, of logs? No, I have a better plan than that. I have a plan of the house of the Lord, given by himself; and you will soon see by this, the difference between our calculations and his idea of things."[8] He then gave them the plan. This was a Saturday night, and on the following Monday work was begun.

For three years the Saints labored with all their strength

45

The Kirtland Temple, first temple built by the Church.

and means to complete the building. The men worked on the walls while the women spun wool and wove it into cloth for clothing. Of these trying days, Joseph's mother writes: "How often I have parted every bed in the house for the accomodation of the brethren, and then laid a single blanket on the floor for my husband and myself, while Joseph and Emma slept upon the same floor, with nothing but their cloaks for both bed and bedding."[9]

In dimension the temple was 59 by 79 feet, 50 feet to the square, and 110 feet to the top of the tower. The walls were built of quarried stone, and the interior was finished with native woods, beautifully worked. No effort was spared to create a house worthy of Deity.

After surveying the building as it stood in 1936, a writer said: "The workmanship, moldings, carvings, etc., show unusual skill in execution. Many motives are used in the various parts, varying in outline, contour and design, but blended harmoniously....It is not probable that all of the workmen engaged on the building were skilled artisans, and yet the result is so harmonious as to raise the question if they may not have been inspired as were the builders of the cathedrals of old."[10]

A Modern Pentecost

The building was completed and ready for dedication March 27, 1836. This was an important day—the climax of three years of toil and sacrifice—and the Saints gathered from far and near. About a thousand of them were able to crowd into the building, and an overflow meeting was held in the schoolhouse.

The services lasted most of the day, from nine in the morning until four in the afternoon, with only a brief recess. The Prophet offered the prayer of dedication, which of itself is an impressive piece of literature. The sacrament of the Lord's supper was then administered.

Since all who desired to participate could not be accommodated at the dedicatory exercises, the services were repeated, and for several days various types of meetings were held in the building, and many spiritual manifestations were experienced. The Prophet compared it with the Day of Pentecost.

The most significant of these experiences occurred on Sunday, April 3. Joseph and Oliver Cowdery were engaged in prayer at the pulpit of the temple, which had been separated from the remainder of the hall by means of curtains. When they had risen from prayer, they beheld a vision, recorded in the Doctrine and Convenants as follows:

"The veil was taken from our minds, and the eyes of our understanding were opened.

"We saw the Lord standing upon the breastwork of the pulpit, before us; and under his feet was a paved work of pure gold, in color like amber.

"His eyes were as a flame of fire; the hair of his head was white like the pure snow; his countenance shone above the brightness of the sun; and his voice was as the sound of the rushing of great waters, even the voice of Jehovah, saying:

"I am the first and the last; I am he who liveth, I am he who was slain; I am your advocate with the Father."[11]

Exodus from Ohio

As the Church grew in numbers and spiritual strength, the forces working against it became more vigorous. Early in the year 1837, a bank was formed in Kirtland, among whose officers were the authorities of the Church. It was only a short time after this that a wave of depression spread over the nation. During the months of March and April, business failures in New York alone passed one hundred million dollars. The Kirtland institution failed along with others, and some of the members of the Church who lost their money in the disaster also lost their faith. It was a dark period in the history of Mormonism.

In the midst of this trouble, elders were called to go to Great Britain to open missionary work there. Heber C. Kimball was appointed to head this mission, and Orson Hyde, Dr. Willard Richards, and Joseph Fielding were called to accompany him. They were to meet John Goodson, Isaac Russell, and John Snyder in New York City, and then proceed to their field of labor.

On June 13, 1837, the Kirtland men left their homes. They had little money and experienced considerable difficulty in reaching Liverpool, where they landed on July 20, 1837. From Liverpool they traveled to Preston, a manufacturing town some thirty miles north, where Joseph Fielding's brother was pastor of Vauxhall Chapel. The missionaries were extended an opportunity to speak in the chapel on the following Sunday. Thus began the work of the Church in the British Isles, which in the years immediately following resulted in the baptism of thousands, many of whom immigrated to the United States and became leaders in the cause.

Meanwhile, in Kirtland, mobbings and the destruction of property by bands of bigoted religionists increased. The Prophet could find no peace, and on January 12, 1838, accompanied by Sidney Rigdon, he left for Missouri, never again to return to Kirtland, where so large and important a part of his work had been done.

6

THE CHURCH IN MISSOURI

WE return to the year 1831. Western Missouri was then a beautiful prairie country of rolling hills and wooded valleys. Its rich soil, pleasing contour, and tolerable climate made it a land of great opportunity. It was only sparsely settled; for instance, Independence, the seat of Jackson County, had only a courthouse, two or three general stores, and a few homes, most of them log cabins.

Joseph Smith indicated to his people that in this area, midway between the Atlantic and the Pacific, they should build their Zion, a city of God.

Their missionaries to the Indians had returned with reports of the nature of the country, and in July 1831, the first group of Saints arrived in western Missouri. About sixty of them had come in a body from Colesville, New York. Twelve miles west of Independence, in what is now part of Kansas City, they laid the foundations of a settlement.

The City of Zion

Other members of the Church soon followed. Joseph Smith, who was then in Missouri, declared that they should acquire by purchase sufficient land that they might live together as a people. He pointed out the site on which they should build a beautiful temple, dedicated to God as his holy house. This should become the crowning glory of the city of Zion.

The Prophet also designed the city. His was a novel and significant concept in civic planning. There would be none of the slums and blighted areas so characteristic of the cities of that day. Nor, on the other hand, would the farmer's family live isolated and alone. This city was to be a mile square, divided into blocks of ten acres with streets 132 feet wide. The center blocks were to be reserved for public buildings. Barns, stables, and farms were to be on the lands adjoining the city. "The tiller of the soil as well as the merchant and mechanic will live in the city," the Prophet said. "The farmer and his family, therefore, will enjoy all the advantages of schools, public lectures and other meetings. His home will no longer be isolated, and his family denied the benefits of society, which has been, and always will be, the great educator of the human race, but they will enjoy the same privileges of society, and can surround their homes with the same intellectual life, the same social refinement as will be found in the home of the merchant or banker or professional man.

"When this square is thus laid off and supplied," the Prophet continued, "lay off another in the same way...and so fill up the world in these last days."[1]

Although there was no opportunity to put the plan in all of its details into operation, its basic principles made possible successful Mormon colonization in the West years later. The common practice of the time was for each man to settle on a large tract of land where he was isolated from his neighbors. But the Mormons undertook the pioneering of new country in groups, building communities in which homes were maintained near church, school, and social centers, with the farms being located outside the town.

Among the first undertakings in the new settlement was the establishment of a printing press for the publication of a periodical, *The Evening and Morning Star,* as well as other literature. Appointed as editor of the *Star* was William W.

Phelps, who, prior to his conversion to Mormonism, had served as editor of a paper in New York. He was a man with considerable literary ability, and his journal soon became a significant force in the community.

The Beginning of Trouble

With bright prospects before them, the Saints set to with a will to build their Zion. But they soon found themselves in serious difficulties. The old settlers resented their religion and their industry. Two ministers were particularly active in creating opposition. The Mormons were pictured as "the common enemies of mankind."[2] Another source of friction was their differences in politics. Most of the Mormons were from the northeastern, anti-slavery states, while Missouri was linked with the South as a pro-slavery state. These and similar differences were enough to arouse the antagonism of the old settlers.

The first real indication of trouble occurred one night in the spring of 1832 when a mob broke windows in a number of Mormon homes. In the autumn of that same year, haystacks were burned and houses were shot into. These acts were but the beginning of a storm of violence that was eventually to sweep the Mormons from the state of Missouri.

In July of 1833 the old settlers, who had been agitated by troublemakers, met in Independence for the purpose of finding means to get rid of the Mormons, "peaceably if we can, forcibly if we must."[3] There was no suggestion that the Mormons had violated any law, simply that they were an evil which had come into their midst, and which had to be removed at all costs. They demanded that no Mormons should henceforth be permitted to settle in Jackson County, that those residing there should promise to move from the county, that they should cease printing their paper, and that other businesses should cease their operations. An ultimatum to this effect was drawn up, and a committee of twelve was detailed to present it to the Mormons.

The meeting was recessed for two hours to allow the committee to present the manifesto and return with an answer.

When notice was served on the Mormons, they were in no position to give an answer. The demands were entirely without legal warrant. The Saints had purchased the ground on which they lived; they had broken no law and had not been accused of breaking any. They were stunned by the whole affair, and they requested three months to consider the matter. This was promptly denied. They then asked for ten days, and were told that fifteen minutes was time enough. Obviously they could not agree to the terms presented them.

Mobocracy

The committee returned to the meeting and reported. The result was a resolution to destroy the printing press. Three days later a mob of five hundred men rode through the streets of Independence, waving a red flag and brandishing pistols, clubs, and whips. They destroyed the press and swore that they would rid Jackson County of the Mormons. Every plea for mercy and justice was met with scoffing. In an effort to save their associates, six of the leading elders of the Church offered themselves as ransom for the Saints. They indicated their willingness to be scourged or even put to death if that would satisfy the mob.

With an oath they were answered that not only they, but all of their associates would be whipped and driven unless they left the county.

Realizing their helplessness, the Mormons agreed under duress that they would evacuate by April 1834. With this understanding the mob dispersed. But it was only a matter of days until they were again breaking into homes and threatening the Saints. Knowing there was no security for them, the Mormons appealed to the governor of the state. He replied that they should take their case to the local courts. Such a suggestion was ridiculous in view of the fact that the judge of the county court, two justices of the peace, and other county officers were leaders of the mob. Nevertheless, the Mormons engaged counsel to present their case.

As might have been expected, the court procedure was without effect, unless it served further to incite the mob. On October 31 a reign of terror commenced. Day and night, armed men rode through the streets of Independence setting fire to houses, destroying furniture, trampling cornfields, whipping and assaulting men and women.

Not knowing where to turn, the inhabitants fled north to the desolate river bottoms. Their trail over the frozen, sleet-covered ground was marked by blood from their lacerated feet. Some lost their lives as a result of exposure and hunger. Fortunately, their brethren in Ohio, on learning of their troubles, brought aid and comfort as rapidly as possible. By the time they arrived, more than two hundred homes had been destroyed. Even more tragic, their dream of Zion had been shattered.

In Upper Missouri

The Saints found temporary refuge in Clay County across the Missouri River opposite Jackson County. To sustain themselves and their families, they worked for the settlers of the area, doing all kinds of labor, from wood chopping to teaching school. Temporary log houses were constructed, in which they lived under wretched conditions until they were able to secure themselves more permanently.

To the northeast of Clay County was a wild, largely unbroken prairie country. They saw in it a land of oppor-

The visitor's center at Independence, Missouri

tunity, and others saw in it a place to put the Mormons where they would be by themselves.

In December 1836, the Missouri legislature created Caldwell County with the thought that it should become a "Mormon county." With characteristic enterprise, the Saints purchased the land and proceeded to lay out cities and farms. Their chief settlement was Far West, and another major colony was planted to the north at Diahman. Two years after the creation of the county, Far West had a population of five thousand, with two hotels, a printing office, blacksmith shops, stores, and 150 houses. Much of this growth had resulted from an influx of Church members from Ohio, including Joseph Smith, who, as we have seen, left Kirtland in January 1838.

The Financial Law of the Church

During this period of intense activity, the Prophet pronounced as a revelation the law of tithing, under which all members were to pay one-tenth of their income to the Church for its work.

This was, of course, only a restatement of an ancient law. In fact, as with other matters of Mormon doctrine and practice, the institution of tithing in 1838 was but a restoration of a principle that had been pronounced in Biblical days. It had been the law of God to his people in Abraham's day and in the times of the prophets who had followed him; and now God had declared anew that his people should be tithed and that this should be "a standing law unto them forever."[4]

A Plague of Sorrow

On July 4, 1838, the Mormons in Far West held a celebration in observance of the nation's Independence Day and the freedom which they then enjoyed from mobs. On this same day, they laid the cornerstone for a new temple. It was to be 110 feet long by 80 feet wide, larger than the structure in Kirtland. Band music and a parade, followed by a reverent dedication, made this day a notable occasion.

But these conditions of peace and progress which they celebrated were to be short-lived. Their old enemies, noting the ever-increasing Mormon population, again sowed dissension. It should be remembered that Missouri was then America's western frontier, and the frontier was generally characterized by a spirit of lawlessness, by the bigotry that comes of ignorance and extremely limited social intercourse, and by suspicion and jealousy. In such an atmosphere it was easy to fan latent fires of intolerance and hatred.

Such agitation led to a conflict in the town of Gallatin on August 6, 1838. It was a minor affair, hardly worthy of notice but for the consequences which followed. A non-Mormon candidate for the state legislature stirred up the old settlers, saying that if the Mormons were allowed to vote, the old settlers would soon lose their rights. It was a simple political contest, but when the Mormons went to cast their ballots, they were forcibly prevented from doing so.

An exaggerated report of the affair reached Far West, and a group of Church members went to investigate. No action was taken, and on their way back to Far West they called at the home of Adam Black, a justice of the peace, and obtained from him a certification to the effect that he was peaceably disposed toward the Mormons and would not attach himself to any mob.

But the enemies of the Saints soon made the most of this trip to Gallatin on the part of the Far West group. Several of them, including this same Justice Black, signed an affidavit to the effect that five hundred armed Mormons had gone into Gallatin to do harm to the non-Mormons of the area. This vicious falsehood was like a match to a pile of straw. Rumor chased rumor until a great fabric of imagined grievances had been built up.

To add to the gravity of the situation, an avowed anti-Mormon of Jackson County days, Lilburn W. Boggs, had become governor. To him the mobocrats sent reports that the Mormons were in insurrection, that they refused to submit to law, and that they were preparing to make war on the old settlers.

Again mobs menacingly rode through the Mormon communities, determined to wage "a war of extermination." When a group of peaceful, non-Mormon citizens appealed to the governor, he is reported to have replied, "The quarrel is between the Mormons and the mob, and they can fight it out."[5]

With such license, trouble spread like a prairie fire before a high wind. When the Mormons tried to defend themselves, the governor used it as an excuse to issue an inhumane and illegal order of extermination—"The Mormons must be treated as enemies, and must be exterminated or driven from the state if necessary for the public peace."[6]

On the 31st day of October, a mob-militia approached the town of Far West. Colonel George M. Hinkle, who led the defenders of the city, requested an interview with General Samuel D. Lucas, commanding the militia. During his interview he agreed to surrender the Mormon leaders without consulting these men. This treachery resulted in the delivery of Joseph Smith, Hyrum Smith, Sidney Rigdon, Parley P. Pratt, and Lyman Wight.

A court-martial was held that night, and the prisoners were sentenced to be shot at sunrise on the public square of Far West. General A. W. Doniphan was ordered to carry out the execution.

To this order Doniphan indignantly replied: "It is cold-blooded murder. I will not obey your order. My brigade shall march for [the town of] Liberty tomorrow morning at 8 o'clock; and if you execute these men, I will hold you responsible before an earthly tribunal, so help me God."[7]

Doniphan was never called to account for this insubordination which saved the Prophet's life. As for the Mormon leader and his fellow prisoners, they were placed in a cramped, dark jail, where they languished for more than five months.

Greatly outnumbered and denied any semblance of legal protection, fifteen thousand members of the Church fled their Missouri homes and property then valued at a million and a half dollars. Through the winter of 1838–39 they painfully made their way eastward toward Illinois, not knowing where else to go. Many died from exposure or from illness aggravated by it. Joseph Smith was in prison, and Brigham Young, a member of the Council of the Twelve Apostles, directed this sorrowful migration, which was to prove to be the forerunner to a yet more tragic movement a scant eight years later, and of which he was to serve as leader.

7

NAUVOO THE BEAUTIFUL

THE people of Quincy, Illinois, received the Mormon refugees with kindness. However, it became quickly apparent to Brigham Young and others that some provision must be made for the settlement of this large group of exiles so that they might again undertake productive enterprise.

On April 22, 1839, Joseph Smith and those who had been imprisoned with him in Liberty, Missouri, arrived in Quincy. Their guards had let them go, and they had made their way to the Illinois side of the Mississippi. The following day a conference was called by the Prophet, and a committee was detailed to investigate the purchase of lands. On May 1 the initial purchase was completed, and other purchases were subsequently made until extensive holdings were secured on both the Iowa and Illinois sides of the river.

The principal location was the site of Commerce, Illinois, about forty-five miles north of Quincy. At this point the river makes a broad bend, giving the land on its east bank the appearance of a promontory. At the time of the purchase, one stone house, three frame houses, and two blockhouses constituted the village.

It was an unhealthy place, so wet that a man had difficulty walking across most of it, and teams became mired to their hips. Of the place and its purchase the Prophet later said, "Commerce was unhealthful, very few could live there; but believing that it might become a healthy place by the blessing of heaven to the Saints, and no more eligible place presenting itself, I considered it wisdom to make an attempt to build up a city."[1]

The Prophet's faith in the future of this site is evident from the name he gave it—Nauvoo, derived from the Hebrew and meaning "the beautiful location."

A Manifestation of God's Power

The swamps were drained, and a city was platted with streets crossing at right angles. But the work of building moved slowly. The people were prostrate, exhausted from the trials through which they had passed. Their energies were depleted, and they became easy victims of malaria.

On the morning of July 22, Joseph, who was sick himself, looked about him only to see others sick. The house in which he lived was crowded with them, and tents sheltering other invalids stood in his dooryard. Wilford Woodruff recounts the events which followed the Prophet's appraisal of this discouraging situation:

"He [Joseph] called upon the Lord in prayer, the power of God rested upon him mightily, and as Jesus healed all the sick around Him in His day, so Joseph, the Prophet of God, healed all around on this occasion. He healed all in his house and dooryard; then, in company with Sidney Rigdon and several of the Twelve, went among the sick lying on the bank of the river, where he commanded them in a loud voice, in the name of Jesus Christ, to rise and be made whole, and they were all healed. When he had healed all on the east side of the river that were sick, he and his companions crossed the Mississippi River in a ferry boat to the west side....The first house they went into was President Brigham Young's. He was sick on his bed at the time. The Prophet went into his house and healed him, and they all came out together.

"As they were passing by my door, Brother Joseph said:

'Brother Woodruff, follow me.' These were the only words spoken by any of the company from the time they left Brother Brigham's house till they crossed the public square, and entered Brother Fordham's house. Brother Fordham had been dying for an hour, and we expected any minute would be his last. I felt the spirit of God that was overpowering his Prophet. When we entered the house, Brother Joseph walked up to Brother Fordham and took him by his right hand, his left hand holding his hat. He saw that Brother Fordham's eyes were glazed, and that he was speechless and unconscious.

"After taking his hand, he looked down into the dying man's face and said '...Do you believe that Jesus is the Christ?' 'I do, Brother Joseph,' was the response. Then the Prophet of God spoke with a loud voice, as in the majesty of Jehovah: 'Elijah, I command you, in the name of Jesus of Nazareth, to rise and be made whole.'

"The words of the Prophet were not like the words of man, but like the voice of God. It seemed to me that the house shook on its foundation. Elijah Fordham leaped from his bed like a man raised from the dead. A healthy color came into his face, and life was manifested in every act. His feet had been done up in Indian meal poultices; he kicked these off, his feet scattered the contents, then called for his clothes and put them on. He asked for a bowl of bread and milk and ate it. He then put on his hat and followed us into the street, to visit others who were sick."[2]

Elijah Fordham lived forty-one years after this experience.

A Mission to England

Even while facing the task of building a city, the Mormons did not neglect the preaching of the gospel. During the summer of 1839, seven members of the Council of the

The city of Nauvoo, built on a promontory on the Mississippi

Twelve Apostles left Nauvoo for England. These men were powerful missionaries. The trials through which they had passed had strengthened their convictions concerning the cause with which they were associated, and they won hundreds of converts through the powerful testimonies which they bore.

Wilford Woodruff's efforts were particularly successful. While preaching in Hanley in the Potteries district of England, he felt impressed to leave that area without knowing why. Obedient to this impression, he traveled to a rural section of Herefordshire. At the home of one John Benbow, a prosperous farmer of the district, he received a cordial welcome and the news that a large group of religionists in that area had broken away from their church and had united themselves to study the scriptures and seek the truth.

Elder Woodruff was given an invitation to speak, and other invitations followed. The organization numbered six hundred, including more than a score of preachers. All of these, with one exception, embraced Mormonism. Before he left the district, eighteen hundred members had been converted to the Church through his efforts.

At a conference held in the British Isles in April 1840, the decision was made to publish an edition of the Book of Mormon, a hymn book, and a periodical.

An unusual mission undertaken during this period was that of Orson Hyde, upon whom the Prophet had once pronounced the blessing: "In due time thou shalt go to Jerusalem, the land of thy fathers, and be a watchman unto the house of Israel; and by thy hand shall the Most High do a work, which shall prepare the way and greatly facilitate the gathering together of that people."[3]

In January 1841, Orson Hyde left the States and went to London, where he labored with other missionaries for some months. Then he made his way to Palestine. Early on the Sunday morning of October 24, 1841, he climbed to the top of the Mount of Olives, and there in prayer and with the authority of the priesthood, he dedicated the land of Palestine for the return of the Jews. The prayer reads in part:

"Grant, therefore, O Lord, in the name of Thy well-beloved Son, Jesus Christ, to remove the barrenness and sterility of this land, and let springs of living water break forth to water its thirsty soil. Let the vine and olive produce in their strength, and the fig-tree bloom and flourish....Let the flocks and the herds greatly increase and multiply upon the mountains and the hills; and let Thy great kindness conquer and subdue the unbelief of Thy people. Do Thou take from them their stony heart, and give them a heart of flesh; and may the Sun of Thy favor dispel the cold mists of darkness which have beclouded their atmosphere....Let kings become their nursing fathers, and queens with motherly fondness wipe the tear of sorrow from their eye." [4]

Following the prayer, he erected a pile of stones as an altar and a witness of his act. With his mission completed, he returned to Nauvoo, arriving in December 1842.

A City from the Swamps

Meanwhile, things had been happening in the western Illinois colony. Homes, shops, and gardens rose from what had been the swamps of Commerce. But because of the extreme poverty in which these people found themselves, their problems were seriously aggravated. Several unsuccessful attempts were made to secure compensation and redress for the losses they had suffered in Missouri. The most notable of these was a petition to the Congress of the United States and an interview between Joseph Smith and the President of the United States, Martin Van Buren.

The petition availed nothing, and Mr. Van Buren replied with a statement that has become famous in Mormon history: "Your cause is just, but I can do nothing for you....If I take up with you I shall lose the vote of Missouri."[5]

The governor of Missouri reacted to these efforts by requesting that the governor of Illinois arrest and deliver to him Joseph Smith and five of his associates as fugitives from justice, although two years had elapsed since they had been allowed to escape from imprisonment in Missouri. The Illinois governor honored the requisition, but on a writ of *habeas corpus* Judge Stephen A. Douglas released the defendants. This action, however, only delayed the Missourians in the execution of their avowed purposes.

The Building of the Temple

During this same period, a decision was made to build a temple in Nauvoo. This sacred edifice was to be reserved for special ordinance work, including baptism for the dead.

The doctrine whereby one who has the opportunity to be baptized is saved, while he who does not have the opportunity is damned, has always appeared discriminatory. And yet the scripture reads, "Except a man be born of water and of the Spirit, he cannot enter into the kingdom of God."[6] The law is all-inclusive.

Joseph Smith resolved this question with the doctrine

The Nauvoo Temple, second temple built by the Mormons. This beautiful structure was desecrated by a mob and later destroyed by fire and storm.

of vicarious baptism for the dead, announcing it as a revelation from God. When performed under proper authority, baptism may be received by living proxies acting in behalf of the dead. Such a practice existed in the primitive Church. This is attested by the words of Paul to the Corinthians: "Else what shall they do which are baptized for the dead, if the dead rise not at all? Why are they then baptized for the dead?"[7]

To provide facilities for such vicarious work, as well as for other sacred ordinances, the Prophet was commanded through revelation to erect a temple. On April 6, 1841, ten thousand members of the Church assembled for the laying of the cornerstones of this structure. By November 8 the baptismal font was completed, and by October 30, 1842, the building had progressed sufficiently to permit the holding of meetings in some rooms. However, it was April 30, 1846, after most of the Saints had left Nauvoo, before it was completed in detail. The building cost approximately one million dollars, and at the time it was regarded as the finest structure in the state of Illinois.

This magnificent edifice stood on the highest elevation of the city and commanded a view of the entire countryside on both sides of the river. It became the crown of Nauvoo, which in itself was remarkable in contrast with most of the frontier towns of America, and which prior to its evacuation was the largest then in Illinois.

Many distinguished visitors called at Nauvoo during this period of intense activity. In 1843 an English writer described the Mormon community in an article which was widely published:

"The city is of great dimensions, laid out in beautiful order; the streets are wide, and cross each other at right angles, which will add greatly to its order and magnificence when finished. The city rises on a gentle incline from the rolling Mississippi, and as you stand near the temple, you may gaze on the picturesque scenery around; at your side is the temple, the wonder of the world; round about, and beneath, you may behold handsome stores, large mansions, and fine cottages, interspersed with varied scenery.... Peace and harmony reign in the city. The drunkard is scarcely even seen, as in other cities, neither does the awful imprecation or profane oath strike upon your ear; but, while all is storm, and tempest, and confusion abroad respecting the Mormons, all is peace and harmony at home."[8]

Colonel Thomas L. Kane visited Nauvoo three years later. His description is particularly interesting:

"Ascending the upper Mississippi in the Autumn, when its waters were low, I was compelled to travel by land past the region of the Rapids.... My eye wearied to see everywhere sordid, vagabond and idle settlers, a country marred, without being improved, by their careless hands.

"I was descending the last hillside upon my journey, when a landscape in delightful contrast broke upon my view. Half encircled by a bend of the river, a beautiful city lay glittering in the fresh morning sun; its bright, new dwellings, set in cool green gardens, ranging up around a stately dome-shaped hill, which was covered by a noble marble edifice, whose high tapering spire was radiant with white and gold. The city appeared to cover several miles; and beyond it, in the background, there rolled off a fair country, chequered by the careful lines of fruitful husbandry. The unmistakeable marks of industry, enterprise and educated wealth everywhere, made the scene one of singular and most striking beauty."[9]

Visitors who came to Nauvoo were impressed with the man under whose direction this remarkable city had risen from disease-ridden swamps. The Prophet at this time was at the zenith of his career. Many of those who knew him during this period have left descriptions of him. He was well-built, about six-feet tall, and weighed approximately two hundred pounds. His eyes were blue, his hair brown and wavy, his skin clear and almost beardless. He was a man of great energy and dignified bearing.

After visiting him, the Masonic grand master of Illinois wrote: "On the subject of religion we widely differed, but he appeared to be quite as willing to permit me to enjoy my right of opinion as I think we all ought to be to let the Mormons enjoy theirs. But instead of the ignorant and tyrannical upstart, judge my surprise at finding him a sensible, intelligent companion and gentlemanly man."[10]

One of the most distinguished men to visit Joseph Smith during this period was Josiah Quincy, who had been mayor of Boston. Out of his impressions of the Prophet he later wrote:

"It is by no means improbable that some future text-book...will contain a question something like this: What historical American of the nineteenth century has exerted the most powerful influence upon the destinies of his countrymen? And it is by no means impossible that the answer to that interrogatory may be thus written: *Joseph Smith, the Mormon Prophet....*

"Born in the lowest ranks of poverty, without book-learning and with the homeliest of human names, he had made himself at the age of thirty-nine a power upon earth. Of all the multitudinous family of Smith, from Adam down (Adam of the 'Wealth of Nations' I mean) none has so won human hearts and shaped human lives as this Joseph."[11]

Such was the reaction of strangers who came to Nauvoo and called upon its most prominent citizen.

In 1839 the Mormons had purchased land so swampy that a horse had difficulty walking across it. By 1844 they had built on this same ground a city without equal on all of the American frontier. Sturdy brick homes, some of which are still occupied, broad farms and orchards, shops, schools, and a magnificent temple—with twenty thousand citizens, gathered not only from the eastern states and Canada, but from the British Isles as well—This was Nauvoo—the Beautiful!

8 THE MARTYRS

On the evening of May 6, 1842, former-governor Lilburn W. Boggs of Missouri was sitting in his home when an unknown assailant fired a pistol through the window and seriously wounded him. The pistol was found on the grounds, but the would-be assassin was not apprehended. It was feared for a time that Boggs would die, but he eventually recovered.

Because he had taken a prominent part in expelling the Mormons from the state, it was soon rumored that they were responsible for the deed. The ex-governor, without any apparent foundation for his act, made an affidavit accusing Orrin Porter Rockwell, a member of the Church, of the crime. He followed this with a second affidavit charging Joseph Smith as accessory-before-the-fact. The governor of Missouri was then asked to requisition the governor of Illinois to deliver Joseph Smith and Rockwell to a representative of the state of Missouri.

A warrant was issued, and the men were arrested; but they were released after trial on a writ of *habeas corpus*. The plans of the Missouri enemies of the Prophet had gone awry, but they were not to be frustrated so easily.

Enemies from Within

In 1840 a Dr. John C. Bennett had allied himself with the Mormon cause. He was a man gifted in many ways, educated and capable, but apparently lacking in principle. Because of his abilities he was given a number of important responsibilities, but when he became involved in moral offenses he was chastised by Joseph Smith. He retaliated by leaving Nauvoo and publishing a book against the Church. He then got in touch with enemies of the Church in Missouri, thus adding fuel to the smoldering fire of hatred. The result of this was another plot for the arrest of Joseph Smith. But, again, this came to nothing.

There was another group in Nauvoo, however, whose efforts were to meet with greater success. Six men—William and Wilson Law, Frances M. and Chauncey L. Higbee, and Charles A. and Robert D. Foster—had been disfellowshipped from the Church, whereupon they determined to retaliate against the Prophet.

Added to these difficulties was the political situation. The Mormons voted for men whose policies they thought would lead to the greatest good, sometimes the candidates of one party and sometimes those of another. In the presidential campaign of 1844, disagreeing with the policies of both major parties, they steered a middle course by nominating Joseph Smith as a candidate for the office of president of the United States, with Sidney Rigdon as a candidate for the vice-presidency. The Mormon leader issued a statement of his views on government which attracted the attention of many. Among other things, he advocated that the government solve the slave problem by purchasing the negroes, thus freeing the slaves and compensating their owners—a policy which if followed might have saved the treasure and lives later sacrificed in the Civil War. He further suggested that prisons be made schools where offenders might be taught useful trades and thus become valuable members of society.

To further acquaint the people of the nation with the Prophet's views, a number of men left Nauvoo to campaign for his candidacy. It was while these men were absent from Nauvoo that the Prophet's troubles reached a climax.

On June 10, 1844, the six men named above published a libelous paper called the *Nauvoo Expositor.* It caused a great stir because it openly maligned prominent citizens of the community.

The people were incensed. Since the Illinois legislature, in the charter given Nauvoo, granted the city the authority "to declare what shall be a nuisance, and to prevent and remove the same,"[1] the city council met for some fourteen hours, took evidence, read the law on the subject of nuisances, consulted the charter granted by the legislature to determine their rights and obligations, declared the publication a nuisance, and ordered the mayor, who was Joseph Smith, to abate it.

He in turn issued an order to the city marshall to "destroy the printing press from whence issues the *Nauvoo Expositor,* and pile the type of said printing establishment in the street, and burn all the *Expositors* and libelous handbills found in said establishment."[2] The marshall carried out the order and so reported.

Its publishers immediately used this as a pretext for accusing Joseph Smith and his brother Hyrum of violating the freedom of the press. They were arrested, tried, and acquitted. But ever since, the action has been denounced by scores of writers. A careful analysis of the law then in effect, however, has led a distinguished legal authority to conclude: "Aside from damages for unnecessary destruction of the press, for which the Nauvoo authorities were unquestionably liable, the remaining actions of the council, including its interpretation of the constitutional guarantee of a free press, can be supported by reference to the law of their day."[3]

But the fire of hatred, which had been fanned so long, now burst into fury. Rumors flew throughout western Illinois. The Prophet's enemies reached Governor Thomas Ford with exaggerated stories, and the governor requested that Joseph and Hyrum meet him in Carthage, where feeling against the Smiths was particularly strong. He added, "I will guarantee the safety of all such persons as may be brought to this place from Nauvoo either for trial or as witnesses for the accused."[4]

To this, Joseph Smith, sensing the real importance of the situation, replied: "We dare not come, though your Excellency promises protection. Yet, at the same time, you have expressed fears that you could not control the mob, in which case we are left to the mercy of the merciless. Sir, we dare not come, for our lives would be in danger, and we are guilty of no crime."[5]

The Prophet knew whereof he spoke. Though he had been arrested and acquitted thirty-seven times, the last entry in his journal, written at this time, reads: "I told Stephen Markham that if I and Hyrum were ever taken again we should be massacred, or I was not a prophet of God."[6]

He thought of escaping to the West, but some of those close to him advised him to go to Carthage and stand trial. To his brother, he said, "We shall be butchered."[7] Nevertheless, on the morning of June 24, 1844, the Prophet and several associates set out for Carthage. Pausing near the temple, they looked at the magnificent building and then at the city, which only five years previous had been little more than swampland. To the group with him Joseph said, "This is the loveliest place and the best people under the heavens; little do they know the trials that await them."[8]

Further on he made another significant remark: "I am

going like a lamb to the slaughter; but I am calm as a summer's morning; I have a conscience void of offense towards God, and towards all men. I shall die innocent, and it shall yet be said of me—he was murdered in cold blood."[9]

When they arrived in Carthage they were arrested on a charge of treason and committed to jail on a false mittimus. When the illegality of this action was protested to Governor Ford, he replied that he did not think it his duty to interfere, as they were in the hands of the law. He thereupon turned the matter over to the local magistrate, who happened to be one of the leaders of the mob, and suggested that he use the Carthage Greys to enforce the incarceration.[10]

Joseph Smith secured an interview with the governor,

Carthage Jail

who promised him that he would be protected from the mobs, which by this time had gathered in Carthage. Moreover, the governor assured him that if he, the governor, went to Nauvoo to investigate matters for himself, as Joseph Smith had requested him to do, he would take the Prophet with him.

Notwithstanding these promises, Governor Ford went to Nauvoo on the morning of June 27, leaving Joseph and Hyrum Smith, and Willard Richards and John Taylor incarcerated in Carthage jail, with a mob militia encamped on the town square.

The day was spent by the prisoners in discussion and the writing of letters. To his wife Joseph wrote: "I am very much resigned to my lot, knowing I am justified, and have done the best that could be done. Give my love to the children...and all who inquire after me....May God bless you all."[11] The letters were sent with visitors who left at one-thirty in the afternoon.

As the day wore on, a feeling of depression came over the group. At the request of the Prophet, John Taylor sang "A Poor Wayfaring Man of Grief," a song dealing with the Savior, which had been popular in Nauvoo.

> A poor, wayfaring man of grief
> Has often crossed me on my way,
> Who sued so humbly for relief
> That I could never answer, Nay.
>
> I had not power to ask his name;
> Whither he went, or whence he came;
> Yet there was something in his eye
> That won my love, I knew not why.

Once when my scanty meal was spread
He entered—not a word he spake!
Just perishing for want of bread;
I gave him all; he blessed it, brake.

* * * *

In prison I saw him next—condemned
To meet a traitor's doom at morn;
The tide of lying tongues I stemmed,
And honored him 'mid shame and scorn.

My friendship's utmost zeal to try
He asked, if I for him would die;
The flesh was weak, my blood ran chill,
But the free spirit cried, "I will."

Then in a moment to my view,
The stranger started from disguise:
The tokens in his hands I knew;
The Savior stood before mine eyes.

He spake—and my poor name he named—
"Of me thou hast not been asham'd;
These deeds shall thy memorial be;
Fear not, thou didst them unto me."

Not long after the song was finished, "there was a little rustling at the outer door of the jail, and a cry of surrender, and also a discharge of three or four firearms followed instantly. The doctor glanced an eye by the window, and saw about a hundred armed men around the door.... The mob encircled the building, and some of them rushed by the guard up the flight of stairs, burst open the door, and began the work of death."

Hyrum was struck first. He fell to the floor exclaiming,

The watch that saved John Taylor's life

"I am a dead man." Joseph ran to him, exclaiming, "Oh, dear brother Hyrum." Then John Taylor was hit, and he fell to the floor seriously wounded. Fortunately, however, the impact of one ball was broken by the watch in his vest pocket. This saved his life.

With bullets bursting through the door, Joseph sprang to the window. Three balls struck him almost simultaneously, two coming from the door and one from the window. Dying, he fell from the open window, exclaiming, "O Lord, my God!"

Dr. Richards escaped without injury, but the Church had lost its Prophet and his brother, the Patriarch. The deed was completed in a matter of seconds.[12]

Sorrow and Hope

When news of the murder of Joseph and Hyrum Smith reached Nauvoo, a pall of gloom settled over the city. The next day the bodies of the dead were taken to Nauvoo. Thousands lined the streets as the cortege passed. The brothers were buried on the following day.

Meanwhile, the inhabitants of Carthage had fled from their homes in fear that the Mormons would rise en masse and wreak vengeance. But there was no disposition to return evil for evil. The Saints were content to leave the murderers in the hands of Him who has said, "Vengeance is mine. I will repay."

The mobocrats had thought that in killing Joseph Smith they had killed Mormonism. But in so doing they had understood neither the character of the people nor the organization of the Church. Joseph had bestowed the keys of authority upon the Apostles, with Brigham Young at their head, and the people sustained them in this capacity, although there was some confusion for a time.

Under the leadership of Brigham Young, the progress of Nauvoo continued. It became increasingly clear, however, that there would be no peace for the Mormons in Illinois. The blood of the Smiths appeared only to have made the mob bolder. The law had not punished the murderers; the governor had apparently connived with them. Why should they not carry to completion the work of extermination?

When the shock of the murders eased, depredations against property began again. Fields of grain were burned, cattle were driven off, then houses on the outskirts of the city were destroyed. Under these circumstances, Brigham Young and other leaders of the Church determined to seek out a place where the Saints could live in peace, unmolested by mobs and prejudiced politicians.

Joseph Smith had uttered a remarkable prophecy in 1842 at a time when the Mormons were enjoying peace in Nauvoo. He had said "that the Saints would continue to suffer much affliction and would be driven to the Rocky Mountains, many would apostatize, others would be put to death by our persecutors or lose their lives in consequence of exposure or disease, and some of you will live to go and assist in making settlements and build cities and see the Saints become a mighty people in the midst of the Rocky Mountains."[13]

There, in the vastness of the West, lay their hope for peace. Constantly badgered by threats and mob force, the Church began preparations in the fall of 1845 to leave their fair city and go forth into the wilderness to find a place where they might finally be able to worship God according to the dictates of their consciences.

9 EXODUS

THE exodus of the Mormons from Nauvoo, Illinois, in February 1846, stands as one of the epic events in the pioneer history of the United States. In severe winter weather, they crossed the Mississippi River, their wagons loaded with the few possessions they could take with them. Behind them were the homes they had constructed from the swamps of Commerce during the seven years they had been permitted to live in Illinois. Before them was the wilderness, largely unknown and uncharted.

Because this march was much like the exodus of the Israelites from their homes in Egypt to a promised land they had not seen, the Mormons named their movement "The Camp of Israel."

Brigham Young and the first company ferried across the river on February 4. A few days later the river froze sufficiently to support teams and wagons. Although this weather proved a boon in expediting the movement, it also brought intense suffering. Of the conditions in which these exiles found themselves, one of their group, Eliza R. Snow, wrote:

"I was informed that on the first night of the encampment, nine children were born into the world, and from that time, as we journeyed onward, mothers gave birth to offspring under almost every variety of circumstances imaginable, except those to which they had been accustomed; some in tents, others in wagons—in rain-storms and in snow-storms....

"Let it be remembered that the mothers of these wilderness-born babies were not savages, accustomed to roam the forest and brave the storm and tempest.... Most of them were born and educated in the Eastern States—had there embraced the gospel as taught by Jesus and his apostles, and, for the sake of their religion, had gathered with the saints, and under trying circumstances had assisted, by their faith, patience and energies, in making Nauvoo what its name indicates, 'the beautiful.' There they had lovely homes, decorated with flowers and enriched with choice fruit trees, just beginning to yield plentifully.

"To these homes, without lease or sale, they had just bid a final adieu, and with what little of their substance could be packed into one, two, and in some instances, three wagons, had started out, desertward, for—where? To this question the only response at that time was, God knows."[1]

Brigham Young presided over this pilgrim band. They accepted him as prophet and leader, the inspired successor to their beloved Joseph. He, they believed, would direct them to a place of refuge "in the midst of the Rocky Mountains," where Joseph had predicted they would become "a mighty people."

Planting for Other Reapers

After the exiles reached the Iowa side of the Mississippi River, they were organized into companies of hundreds, and standards of conduct were set up. The companies were subdivided into fifties and tens, with officers over each group. Brigham Young was sustained as "president over the whole Camp of Israel."[2]

They traveled in a northwesterly direction, over the territory of Iowa, through a sparsely-settled region between the Mississippi and Missouri Rivers. In the early days of their movement, snow lay on the ground to a depth of six or eight inches, and their canvas wagon covers offered little protection against the cold north winds.

With the coming of spring, the snow melted, making travel even more difficult. There were no roads in the direction the Saints traveled; they had to build their own. At times the mud was so deep that three yoke of oxen were required to pull a load of five hundred pounds. Exhausted by a day of pushing and pulling, chopping wood for bridges, loading and unloading wagons, the travelers would find they had moved only a half dozen miles. Slush and rain

Crossing the Mississippi

made their camps veritable quagmires. Exposure to such conditions, together with improper nourishment, took a heavy toll of life.

Burials along the way were frequent. Crude coffins were fashioned from cottonwood trees, brief services were held, and the loved ones of the deceased turned their faces and their teams westward, realizing they would never pass this way again. One wonders why these people did not become bitter and vindictive, particularly when they remembered their comfortable homes now ravaged and burned by the Illinois mob.

But they lightened their sorrows with self-made pleasures. They had their own brass band, and they made good use of it. The settlers of Iowa were often amazed to see these pioneers clear a piece of land about their camp fires, and then dance and sing until the bugler sounded taps.

It was while traveling under these circumstances that one of their number, William Clayton, composed that epic hymn of the prairie, "Come, Come Ye Saints." Set to an old English air, this song became an anthem of hope and faith for all the thousands of Mormon pioneers. Nothing, perhaps, expresses so well the spirit of this movement.

When food became scarce, the pioneers found it necessary to trade precious possessions—dishes, silverware, lace—brought from the East or across the sea, for a little corn and salt pork. In this way the homes of many Iowa settlers were made more attractive and the Mormons were able to replenish their scant food supplies. Occasionally the brass band traveled out of its way a considerable distance to give a concert in a frontier settlement in order to add to the commissary.

One of the remarkable features of this movement was the building of temporary settlements along the way. The

Come, Come, Ye Saints

William Clayton
Resolutely ♩= 66

Old English Tune

1. Come, come, ye Saints, no toil nor la-bor fear; But with joy
2. Why should we mourn or think our lot is hard? 'Tis not so;
3. We'll find the place which God for us pre-pared, Far a-way
4. And should we die be-fore our jour-ney's through, Hap-py day!

wend your way. Though hard to you this jour-ney may ap-pear,
all is right. Why should we think to earn a great re-ward,
in the West, Where none shall come to hurt or make a-fraid;
all is well! We then are free from toil and sor-row, too;

Grace shall be as your day. 'Tis bet-ter far for
If we now shun the fight? Gird up your loins; fresh
There the Saints will be blessed. We'll make the air with
With the just we shall dwell! But if our lives are

us to strive Our use-less cares from us to drive; Do
cour-age take; Our God will nev-er us for-sake; And
mu-sic ring, Shout prais-es to our God and King; A-
spared a-gain To see the Saints their rest ob-tain, O

this, and joy your hearts will swell— All is well! all is well!
soon we'll have this tale to tell— All is well! all is well!
bove the rest these words we'll tell— All is well! all is well!
how we'll make this cho-rus swell— All is well! all is well!

pioneer company occasionally stopped long enough to clear, fence, plow, and plant large sections of ground. The leaders called for volunteers—some to split rails for fences and bridges, others to remove trees, and others to plow and sow. A few cabins were built, and several families were detailed to remain and care for the crops. Then the pioneer company moved forward, leaving the crops for later companies to harvest.

This spirit of mutual service and cooperation characterized the entire movement. Without this, the migration of twenty thousand people through the wilderness could have ended in disaster.

Approximately three and a half months after leaving Sugar Creek, their camp on the west shore of the Mississippi, the pioneer company reached Council Bluffs on the Missouri. Following them, across the entire territory of Iowa, was a slow-moving train of hundreds of wagons. They were to continue to filter out of Nauvoo and move over the rolling Iowa hills all of that summer and late into the year. Here was modern Israel seeking a new promised land!

The Mormon Battalion

On a June morning in 1846, at one of the temporary camps along the trail, the Mormons were surprised by the approach of a platoon of United States soldiers. Captain James Allen had come with a call for five hundred able young men to fight in the war with Mexico.

He was directed on to Council Bluffs to see Brigham Young and other authorities of the Church. It is not surprising that the leaders remarked on the irony of the situation—their country, which had stood by while they, its citizens, had been dispossessed of their homes by unconstitutional mobs, now called upon them for military volunteers.

It is true that the Mormons had petitioned the government for assistance in the form of contracts to build block-houses along the westward trail. They believed that this would be a service to the thousands of emigrants, Mormon and non-Mormon, who would move west in the years to come. Such blockhouses would afford protection against the Indians and other dangers of the prairie. But a military call for five hundred urgently-needed men was hardly the answer they expected. Moreover, the call was highly disproportionate in terms of numbers when compared with the population of the nation as a whole.

Nevertheless, they responded. Brigham Young and others went from camp to camp, hoisting the national flag at each recruiting place. And though this meant leaving families fatherless on the plains, the men enlisted when President Young assured them that their families should have food so long as his own had any.

Captain Allen expressed amazement at the music and dancing on the eve of departure. The recruits were to go to Mexico. Their families now of necessity would be compelled to establish winter quarters and wait until the following year to go to the Rocky Mountains. When or where they would meet again was an open question. Perhaps it was a statement from Brigham Young that eased the sorrow of departure. He promised the men that "if they would perform their duties faithfully, without murmuring and go in the name of the Lord, be humble, and pray every morning and evening" they would not have to fight and would return home safely.[3]

From Council Bluffs the Mormon Battalion marched to Fort Leavenworth. There they received advance pay for clothing, and a large part of this money they sent back for the relief of their families.

From Leavenworth they marched southwest to the old

The Mormon Battalion Monument erected on the Utah state capitol grounds

Spanish town of Santa Fe. Here they were saluted by the garrison under the command of Colonel Alexander W. Doniphan, the man who had saved Joseph Smith's life in Missouri.

From Santa Fe they marched south down the valley of the Rio Grande, but before reaching El Paso they turned to the west, following the San Pedro River.

They then crossed the Gila River, marched to Tucson, followed the Gila to the Colorado, and made their way over the mountains to San Diego, California. Much of the road they made was later followed by the Southern Pacific Railroad.

The story of their historic march is one of suffering from insufficient rations, of killing thirst and desperate attempts to secure water, of exhausting travel through heavy desert sand, and of cutting a road over forbidding mountains. They had left their families in June 1846. They reached San Diego January 29, 1847. The war was over when they reached their post, and they were not obliged to do any fighting. Brigham Young's prophetic promise had been fulfilled.

Upon reaching the Pacific Coast, their commander, Colonel Philip St. George Cooke of the United States Army, congratulated them with a citation, which reads in part as follows:

"The lieutenant colonel commanding, congratulates the battalion on their safe arrival on the shore of the Pacific Ocean, and the conclusion of their march of over two thousand miles.

"History may be searched in vain for an equal march of infantry. Half of it has been through a wilderness, where nothing but savages and wild beasts are found, or deserts where, for want of water, there is no living creature. There, with almost hopeless labor, we have dug deep wells, which the future traveler will enjoy. Without a guide who had traversed them we have ventured into trackless tablelands where water was not found for several marches. With crowbar and pick and axe in hand, we have worked our way over mountains, which seemed to defy aught save the wild goat, and hewed a pass through a chasm of living rock more narrow than our wagons."[4]

But while the members of the Battalion had been serving under their country's flag, those of their people who had remained in Nauvoo were being driven by mobs in defiance of every constitutional guarantee.

The Fall of a City

Although most of the Mormons had succeeded in getting out of Nauvoo before May 1, 1846, the date set by the mob for their complete departure, some of their number had not been so fortunate. By August there remained about one thousand, many of them sick and aged. It was thought that the mob would spare these, at least.

But history bears somber witness of the fact that those who had indulged in such wishful thinking were mistaken.

When it became apparent that the mob would not wait, the people of Nauvoo appealed to the governor for aid. He responded by sending a Major Parker with ten men to represent the militia of the state of Illinois. Major Parker was later succeeded by a Major Clifford.

The mob answered the Major's appeals for a peaceful settlement of the difficulty by attacking him and the Mormons who had volunteered to serve under him. Though greatly outnumbered, the defenders of the city fashioned five old steamboat shafts into cannons and constructed improvised breastworks. In the name of the people of Illinois, Major Clifford requested the mobbers to disperse.

Their answer was an assault on the city. The defenders were able to hold them off for a time, but they were so seriously outnumbered that the Mormons had no choice but to agree to evacuate the city as quickly as they could gather together a few of their possessions.

Even this did not satisfy the mob. While the Mormons

were leaving, they were set upon and abused, and their wagons were ransacked for anything of value. Crossing to the Iowa side of the river, they set up a temporary camp. Colonel Thomas L. Kane of Philadelphia, who chanced to see them at this time, later described their situation before the Historical Society of Pennsylvania:

"Dreadful, indeed, was the suffering of these forsaken beings. Cowed and cramped by cold and sunburn, alternating as each weary day and night dragged on, they were, almost all of them, the crippled victims of disease. They were there because they had no homes, nor hospital nor poor-house nor friends to offer them any. They could not satisfy the feeble cravings of their sick: they had not bread to quiet the fractious hunger-cries of their children....

"These were Mormons, famishing in Lee County, Iowa, in the fourth week of the month of September, in the year of our Lord 1846. The city [which he had just visited],—it was Nauvoo, Illinois. The Mormons were the owners of that city, and the smiling country around. And those who had stopped their ploughs, who had silenced their hammers, their axes, their shuttles and their workshop wheels; those who had put out their fires, who had eaten their food, spoiled their orchards, and trampled under foot their thousands of acres of unharvested bread; these,—were the keepers of their dwellings, the carousers in their temple,—whose drunken riot insulted the ears of their dying."[5]

In these straitened conditions, many would doubtless have starved but for thousands of quail which flew into their camp, and which they were able to catch with their hands. These they regarded as manna from heaven, an answer to prayer.

Fortunately, they were not left in this condition for long. Their brethren, who had gone on ahead, sent back relief wagons and divided with them their own meager stores. Their last picture of Nauvoo, as they tediously made their way over the Iowa hills, was of the tower of their sacred temple, now spoiled and desecrated.

10 TO THE PROMISED LAND

It was apparent to Brigham Young and the other leaders of the Church that it would be unwise to attempt to reach the Rocky Mountains in the year 1846, since the expedition now had been seriously weakened by the loss of the young men who had marched with the Mormon Battalion. Accordingly, a temporary settlement was established along the Missouri River.

The site, adjoining the present city of Omaha, soon had more of the appearance of a town than a camp. Many of the people got along with dugouts and other crude shelters. However, a thousand sturdy log houses were erected before January 1847.

During all of that winter, feverish activity went on. Anvils rang with the making and repairing of wagons. Available maps and reports were carefully studied, and every preparation possible was undertaken to ensure the success of the move scheduled for the following spring.

The community was not without its pleasures, although comforts were few. Dances were frequently held under the sponsorship of the various quorums of the priesthood. Religious worship was carried on as though the people were permanently settled. Schools for the children were successfully conducted, for the education of the young has always been of prime importance in Mormon philosophy.

But often a pupil—sometimes several—did not appear when the school bell rang. A type of scurvy, called black

*Monument to the Utah pioneers in the old cemetery at
Winter Quarters*

canker, took a sorrowful toll. Lack of proper nourishment, insufficient shelter, extremes of temperature in the lowlands along the river—these made the people easy victims of disease.

In recent years the Church has erected a monument in the old cemetery of Winter Quarters. In heroic size it depicts a mother and father laying a child in a grave they know they never again will visit. Surrounding the monument are the graves of some six hundred of those who died at this temporary encampment on the prairie.

Westward

In the early spring of 1847, plans were completed for the sending of a pioneer company to the Rocky Mountains. Their responsibility was to chart a route and find a place for the thousands who would follow.

On January 14, President Young delivered to the Saints what he declared to be a revelation from the Lord. This became the constitution governing their westward movement. It is an interesting document, reading in part as follows:

"The Word and Will of the Lord concerning the Camp of Israel in their journeyings to the West:

"Let all of the people of the Church of Jesus Christ of Latter-day Saints, and those who journey with them, be organized into companies, with a covenant and promise to keep all the commandments and statutes of the Lord our God.

"Let all the companies be organized with captains of hundreds, captains of fifties, and captains of tens, with a president and his two counselors at their head, under the direction of the Twelve Apostles.

"And this shall be our covenant—that we will walk in all the ordinances of the Lord....

"And if any man shall seek to build up himself, and seeketh not my counsel, he shall have no power, and his folly shall be made manifest.

"Seek ye; and keep all your pledges one with another; and covet not that which is thy brother's.

"Keep yourselves from evil to take the name of the Lord in vain....

"Cease to contend one with another, cease to speak evil one of another.

"Cease drunkenness, and let your words tend to edifying one another.

"If thou borrowest of thy neighbor, thou shalt return that which thou hast borrowed; and if thou canst not repay then go straightway and tell thy neighbor, lest he condemn thee.

"If thou shalt find that which thy neighbor hast lost, thou shalt make diligent search till thou shalt deliver it to him again.

"Thou shalt be diligent in preserving that which thou hast, that thou mayest be a wise steward; for it is the free gift of the Lord thy God, and thou art his steward.

"If thou art merry, praise the Lord with singing, with music, with dancing, and with a prayer of praise and thanksgiving.

"If thou art sorrowful, call on the Lord thy God with supplication, that your souls may be joyful.

"Fear not thine enemies, for they are in mine hands, and I will do my pleasure with them."[1]

To these general standards of conduct were added other specific rules. Every man was to carry a loaded gun or have one in his wagon where, in case of attack, he could get it at a moment's notice. At night the wagons were to be drawn into a circle to form a corral for the teams. There was to be no travel or work on the Sabbath; both teams and men should rest on that day. Prayer, night and morning, should be a regular practice in the camp.

On April 5 the pioneer company started west. It consisted of 143 men, 3 women, and 2 children, with Brigham Young leading the group. Fortunately, when they had gone only a short distance, Apostles Parley P. Pratt and John Taylor arrived at Winter Quarters from England. They brought with them barometers, sextants, telescopes, and other instruments. In the hands of Orson Pratt, an accomplished scientist, these made it possible for the pioneers to determine the latitude, longitude, temperature, and elevation above sea level of their position each day. Such information was invaluable in the preparation of a guide for those who were to come later.

One of the famous trails of history already existed along the south side of the Platte River. It was to become more heavily traveled in years to come by thousands of emigrants bound for Oregon and California. However, Brigham Young decided against using the Oregon road, and determined to break a new trail on the north side of the river. In so doing, he said, the Mormons would avoid conflict with other westward-bound people and would also have more feed for the cattle of the companies to follow. It is interesting to note that when the Union Pacific Railroad was built some years later, it followed this Mormon road for a considerable distance.

In 1847 great herds of buffalo roamed the plains. It was customary practice among westward-bound emigrants to shoot them simply for sport. But Brigham Young took a different attitude. He advised his people to kill no more than were needed for meat.

A Log of the Journey

For a number of reasons, not the least of which was to prepare a guide for those to come later, the pioneers were interested in knowing the number of miles they covered each day. The first device employed to determine this was a red cloth tied to a wagon wheel. By counting the revolutions of the wheel and multiplying this number by the circumference of the rim, it was possible to determine the distance traveled. But watching the revolutions of a wheel, day in and day out, soon became tedious. There was need for a better way.

Consulting with Orson Pratt, Appleton Harmon solved the problem. Carving a set of wooden gears, he constructed what was called a roadometer. It was a novel device, the forerunner of the modern odometer. Although constructed of wood, it was amazingly accurate.

For the guidance of those who should follow, the pioneer company left letters describing mileage and conditions of the trail. These were tucked in an improvised mail box or were painted on a sun-bleached buffalo skull.

Journals were carefully kept, noting details of the journey. Two excerpts from Orson Pratt's journal serve as illustrations:

"*May 22nd.*—At a quarter past five this morning, the barometer stood at 26.623, attached thermometer at 51.5 degrees, detached thermometer 48.5 degrees. A light breeze from the south—the sky partially overspread with thin clouds.... Five and a half miles from our morning encampment we crossed a stream, which we named Crab Creek; one and three-quarters mile further we halted for noon. A meridian observation of the sun placed us in latitude 41 deg. 30 min. 3 sec. I intended to have taken a lunar distance for the longitude, but clouds prevented. With our

*The wooden odometer that measured the daily distance
traveled by the pioneer wagons*

glasses, Chimney Rock can now be seen at a distance of 42
miles up the river. At this distance it appears like a short
tower placed upon an elevated mound or hill. Four and a
quarter miles further brought us to another place where the
river strikes the bluffs; as usual we were obliged to pass over
them, and in about two and a quarter miles we again came
to the prairie bottoms, and driving a short distance we
encamped, having made fifteen and a half miles during the
day. For a number of miles past, the formation, more particularly that of the bluffs, has been gradually changing
from sand to marl and soft earthy limestone, the nature of

99

which is beginning to change the face of the country, presenting scenes of remarkable picturesque beauty....

"*May 23rd.*—To-day, as usual, we let ourselves and teams rest. The mercury in the barometer is, this morning, much more depressed than what can be accounted for by our gradual ascent; at five o'clock it stood at 26.191, attached thermometer 54.5 deg., detached thermometer 52 deg. A depression of the mercury is said to indicate high winds. To-day several of us again visited the tops of some of these bluffs, and by a barometrical measurement I ascertained the height of one [of] them to be 235 feet above the river, and 3590 feet above the level of the sea.... Rattlesnakes are very plentiful here.... Soon after dinner we attended public worship, when the people were interestingly and intelligently addressed by President B. Young and others."[2]

The route of the pioneers lay up the valley of the Platte to the confluence of the North Platte and South Platte Rivers. It then followed the North Platte through what is now Nebraska and Wyoming to a point where the Sweetwater River flows into the North Platte. The route then lay along this stream to its headwaters near South Pass, Wyoming.

By June 1 the company had reached old Fort Laramie, where they were surprised to find a group of Church members from Mississippi who had come from the south by way of Pueblo, Colorado, with the purpose of joining the pioneer company and following them to their destination.

On June 27 they moved over South Pass, that place where the Rockies gently slope to the prairie, and over which moved most of the westward-bound emigrants. At South Pass the Mormons met Major Moses Harris, a famous trapper and scout. From him they received a description of the basin of the Salt Lake. His report of the country was

A replica of one of the buffalo skulls left for the guidance of groups who followed the original company of pioneers

unfavorable. Of this interview Orson Pratt wrote:

"We obtained much information from him in relation to the great interior basin of the Salt Lake, the country of our destination. His report, like that of Captain Fremont's, is rather unfavourable to the formation of a colony in this basin, principally on account of the scarcity of timber. He said that he had travelled the whole circumference of the lake, and that there was no outlet to it."[3]

On June 28 they met that wiry veteran of the west, Jim Bridger. Anxious to learn all they could of the country

101

toward which they were traveling, the Mormons accepted his suggestion that they make camp and spend the night with him. He indicated that some good country could be found both to the north and to the south of the basin of the Salt Lake, but he discouraged any plan for establishing a large colony in the basin itself.

On June 30 Samuel Brannan rode into view. He was a member of the Church who, on February 4, 1846, the date of the first exodus from Nauvoo, had sailed from New York with more than two hundred Mormons bound for California by way of Cape Horn. Landing at Yerba Buena, now San Francisco, he had established the first English-language newspaper published there. He left California in April, riding east over the mountains to meet Brigham Young. Enroute he had passed the scene of the Donner Party tragedy of the preceding winter, and gave the Mormons a description of that ill-fated camp in which more than a score of people starved to death in the snows of the Sierras. Brannan enthusiastically described for President Young the beauties of California. It was, he indicated, a rich and productive land of great beauty and equable climate, a land where the Mormons could prosper. But President Young could not be dissuaded from the purpose to which he had set himself— God had a place for his people, and there they would go to work out their destiny.

"This Is the Right Place"

As the pioneer company approached the mountains, travel became more difficult. Their teams were jaded, and their wagons were worn. Moreover, the steep mountain canyons, with their swift streams, huge boulders, and heavy tree growth, presented problems very different from those experienced on the plains.

On July 21 Orson Pratt and Erastus Snow, two advance

Great Salt Lake City as it appeared in 1853

scouts, entered the Salt Lake Valley. Three days later Brigham Young, who had moved more slowly because of illness, rode out of the canyon and looked across the valley. He paused, and then announced, "This is the right place."

This was the promised land! This valley with its salty lake gleaming in the July sun. This treeless prairie in the mountains. This tract of dry land broken only by a few bubbling streams running from the canyons to the lake. This was the object of vision and of prophecy, the land of which thousands yet at Winter Quarters dreamed. This was their land of refuge, the place where the Saints would "become a mighty people in the midst of the Rocky Mountains."

11 PIONEERING THE WILDERNESS

Two hours after the arrival of the main body of pioneers, the first plowing in the Salt Lake Valley was undertaken. The ground, however, was so dry and hard that the plows were broken. Consequently, one of the canyon streams was diverted and the soil soaked. Thereafter the plowing was easier. On July 24 potatoes were planted and the ground watered. This was the beginning of irrigation by Anglo-saxon people in the West, marking, in fact, the beginning of modern irrigation practice.

Although other seeds were also planted in addition to the potatoes, there was small chance that a crop of any consequence would mature. But it was hoped that at least enough of a crop would develop to provide seed for the following spring.

Brigham Young arrived on Saturday, and on the following day the people met for worship. There they received a statement of the policies that were to prevail in the new colony. President Young declared that no work should be done on Sunday. He promised that if it was, the offender would discover that he would lose five times as much as he gained. No one was to hunt on that day. No man was to try to buy land, but every man would have his land measured out to him for city and farming purposes. He could till it as he pleased, but he must be industrious and take care of it. There was to be no private ownership of streams of water, and wood and timber were to be regarded as common property. President Young also advised the Saints to use only dead timber for fuel in order to save the live timber for future use. He promised that if they would walk faithfully in the light of these laws they would be a prosperous people.[1]

The First Winter

The next day everyone was busy exploring the surrounding country to learn of its resources. Though their faith was strong and their hopes high, the situation in which these people found themselves was anything but encouraging. They were a small group with scant provisions, located a thousand miles from the nearest settlement to the east and seven hundred miles from the Pacific Coast. They were unfamiliar with the resources of this strange new land, which was untried and different in its nature from that which they had left.

Yet they began preparations for an extensive city. Four days after their arrival in the valley, Brigham Young walked to a spot north of their camp and proclaimed, "Here is the [place] for our temple."[2] The city was soon platted around this site, with streets 132 feet wide. Such width was considered foolish in those days, but the foresight in this action has become evident with the advent of modern traffic. The projected community was named Great Salt Lake City.

One thing that caught the fancy of the pioneers as they explored the valley was the similarity between this new-found Zion and the Holy Land. Twenty-five miles south of their camp was a beautiful fresh water lake with a river running from it to the Great Salt Lake, another Dead Sea. They named the river Jordan.

Once policies and plans had been decided, Brigham Young and others began the long journey back to Winter Quarters. Those remaining in the valley immediately commenced construction of a fort in which to house themselves as well as the large company expected later in the summer. Most of the families spent the first winter in the fort, although there were a few who ventured to build homes of their own.

Fortunately, that first winter was unusually mild. Nevertheless, the colonists suffered. Food was poor and scarce, as was clothing. Sego roots were dug and thistle tops were boiled for food. In remembrance of the part it played in sustaining life, the sego lily is today Utah's state flower.

No time was wasted in preparing for the future. All through the winter the task of fencing and clearing the land progressed. A common field of five thousand acres was plowed and planted. This was a tremendous accomplishment, considering the tools these people had.

The Coming of the Gulls

In the spring, wide fields of green grain appeared to be ample reward for the labors of the previous fall and winter. Now, these people thought, there would be plenty to eat, both for themselves and for the large number of immigrants expected that summer. Under irrigation, the crops flourished. The future looked bright.

Then one day it was noticed that large crickets were eating the grain. These had been seen by the first men to enter the valley, and the newcomers had noted that some of the natives used them for food. But they had expected nothing of this kind. Each day the situation grew worse. The insects came in myriads, devouring everything before them.

Terror struck into the hearts of the people as they saw their grain fall before the insects. With all their strength they fought them. They tried burning and drowning. They tried beating them with shovels and brooms. They tried every means they could devise to save their crops. Still the voracious insects came, eating every stalk of grain before them.

Exhausted and in desperation, the Saints turned to the Lord, pleading in prayer for preservation of bread for their children.

Then, to their amazement, they saw great flocks of white-winged sea gulls flying from over the lake to the west

Monument on Temple Square honoring the miracle of the sea gulls

and settling on the fields. At first the people thought they were coming to add to the devastation. But the gulls went after the crickets, devouring them, then flying away and disgorging, only to return for more.

The crops of 1848 were saved, and on Temple Square in Salt Lake City stands a monument to the sea gull. In bronze it bears the inscription, "Erected in grateful remembrance of the mercy of God to the Mormon Pioneers."

Gold in California

Brigham Young returned to Winter Quarters on October 31, 1847. On the following December 5, he was sustained as President of the Church. From the time of Joseph Smith's death, Brigham had led the Church in his capacity as President of the Council of Twelve Apostles. He named as his counselors in the First Presidency Heber C. Kimball, who had come into the Church with him, and Dr. Willard Richards.

On May 26, 1848, he left Winter Quarters, never again to return to the East. While he now knew the way, this second journey was more difficult than had been the pioneer trip. The company of which he was leader included "397 wagons with 1229 souls, 74 horses, 19 mules, 1275 oxen, 699 cows, 184 cattle, 411 sheep, 141 pigs, 605 chickens, 37 cats, 82 dogs, 3 goats, 10 geese, 2 beehives, 8 doves, and 1 crow."[3] It was no small task to shepherd such a caravan over a thousand miles of prairie and mountains.

They reached the valley on October 20, 116 days after their departure from Winter Quarters. Meanwhile, something had happened in California that had fired the hearts of the adventurous the world over, and that was to have its effect on the Mormons.

After the Mormon Battalion had been mustered out in California, some of the Battalion men stopped at Sutter's

Fort in the Sacramento Valley to work and earn a little money before crossing the mountains to rejoin their families. Six of them, with Sutter's foreman, James W. Marshall, and some Indians, undertook the construction of a sawmill on the south fork of the American River. There, on January 24, 1848, Marshall picked some gold out of the sand in the mill race. Henry Bigler, one of the Battalion men, wrote in his journal that night: "This day some kind of metal was found in the tail race that looks like gold."[4]

This historic entry is the only original documentation of the discovery that sent men rushing over land and sea to California.

But while others were rushing to the American River, the Battalion men completed their contract with Sutter, gathered together what possessions they had, and made their way east over the mountains to the semi-arid valley of the Great Salt Lake, there to undertake with their friends the painful labor of subduing the wilderness.

Meanwhile, the gold fever had infected some of those in the valley who had just passed through a difficult winter. Speaking of this, Brigham Young said:

"Some have asked me about going. I have told them that God has appointed this place for the gathering of his Saints, and you will do better right here than you will by going to the gold mines.... Those who stop here and are faithful to God and his people will make more money and get richer than you that run after the god of this world; and I promise you in the name of the Lord that many of you that go thinking you will get rich and come back, will wish you had never gone away from here, and will long to come back, but will not be able to do so. Some of you will come back, but your friends who remain here will have to help you; and the rest of you who are spared to return will not make as much money as your brethren do who stay here and help build up the Church and Kingdom of God; they will prosper and be able to buy you twice over. Here is the place God has appointed for his people....

"...As the Saints gather here and get strong enough to possess the land, God will temper the climate, and we shall build a city and a temple to the Most High God in this place. We will extend our cities and our settlements to the east and the west, to the north and to the south, and we will build towns and cities by the hundreds, and thousands of the Saints will gather from the nations of the earth. This will become the great highway of the nations. Kings and emperors and the noble and wise of the earth will visit us here, while the wicked and ungodly will envy us our comfortable homes and possessions. Take courage, brethren.... Plow your land and sow wheat, plant your potatoes.... The worst fear that I have about this people is that they will get rich in this country, forget God and his people, wax fat, and kick themselves out of the Church and go to hell. This people will stand mobbing, robbing, poverty and all manner of persecution, and be true. But my greater fear for them is that they cannot stand wealth; and yet they have to be tried with riches, for they will become the richest people on this earth."[5]

Before the close of the year 1848 the population of the valley had reached five thousand. This heavy influx of immigrants seriously taxed the resources of the community. Hunger and hardship were common that winter, and these circumstances added to the discouragement of many. In the midst of these trying conditions, Heber C. Kimball, speaking before the people in one of their meetings, prophesied that in less than one year there would be plenty of clothing and other needed articles sold on the streets of Salt

Lake City for less than in New York or St. Louis.[6]

Such a situation was incredible, but the fulfillment of that prophecy came about, and in remarkable fashion.

Thinking to get rich with the sale of goods in California, eastern merchants had loaded great wagon trains with clothing, tools, and other items for which there would be demand at the gold diggings. But on reaching Salt Lake City they learned that competitors had beaten them by shipping around the Cape.

Their only interest then was to unload what they had for what price they could get and go on to California as quickly as possible. Auctions were held from their wagons on the streets of Salt Lake City. Cloth and clothing sold for less than they could be bought for in New York. Badly needed tools could be had for less than in St. Louis. Fine teams, jaded from the long journey, were eagerly traded for the fatter but less valuable stock of the Mormons. Good, heavy wagons, in great demand in the mountain colony, were traded for lighter vehicles in which the gold seekers could make better time.

Glad Tidings to the World

While eager men were traveling over land and sea to search for gold, the Mormons also sent eager men over land and sea—in search of souls. Missionaries were sent to the Eastern States, to Canada, and to the British Isles. In spite of the prejudices that moved before them, they made substantial headway with the baptism of thousands of souls.

Missionary work in France and Italy was not so fruitful, although some converts were made at first. In the Scandinavian countries, the elders were mobbed and jailed, but a spirit of tolerance gradually developed, and thousands of converts were made in those lands.

These preachers, traveling without purse or scrip, went

to Malta, to India, to Chile, and to the islands of the Pacific. Almost everywhere they encountered hatred and the cries of the mob. But in all of these lands they found a few who were receptive to their message.

Once baptized, these converts desired almost invariably to "gather" with others of their faith in the valleys of the Rockies—Zion, they called it. And once there, differences of language and customs were soon lost sight of as men and women from many lands worked together in the building of a commonwealth.

Zion Spreads Her Branches

It was inevitable that the boundaries of the Church should extend beyond the valley of the Salt Lake. With thousands of converts coming from the nations, other settlements were founded. At first these were rather close to the mother colony, but soon wagon trains were moving north and south toward the distant valleys. By the close of the third year, settlements extended two hundred miles to the south. By the end of the fourth year, colonies were found over a distance of three hundred miles. Then, in 1851, five hundred of the Saints were called to go to southern California to plant a colony. They there laid the foundations of San Bernardino.

In nearly every case this pioneering entailed great sacrifice. Families were often called to leave their comfortable homes and cultivated fields and go into the wilderness to begin over again. But through their efforts hundreds of colonies were planted over a vast section of the West. Of the extent of this colonization, James H. McClintock, Arizona state historian, wrote:

"It is a fact little appreciated that the Mormons have been first in agricultural colonization of nearly all the intermountain States of today.... Not drawn by visions of wealth, unless they looked forward to celestial mansions, they sought, particularly, valleys wherein peace and plenty could be secured by labor....

"First of the faith on the western slopes of the continent was the settlement at San Francisco by Mormons from the ship Brooklyn. They landed July 21, 1846, to found the first English speaking community of the Golden State, theretofore Mexican. These Mormons established the farming community of New Helvetia, in the San Joaquin Valley, the same fall, while men from the Mormon Battalion, January 24, 1848, participated in the discovery of gold at Sutter's Fort. Mormons also were pioneers in Southern California, where in 1851, several hundred families of the faith settled at San Bernardino.

"The first Anglo-Saxon settlement within the boundaries of the present State of Colorado was at Pueblo, November 15, 1846, by Capt. James Brown and about 150 Mormon men and women who had been sent back from New Mexico, into which they had gone, a part of the Mormon Battalion that marched on to the Pacific Coast.

"The first American settlement in Nevada was one of the Mormons in the Carson Valley, at Genoa, in 1851.

"In Wyoming, as early as 1854, was a Mormon settlement at Green River, near Fort Bridger, known as Fort Supply.

"In Idaho, too, preeminence is claimed by virtue of a Mormon settlement at Fort Lemhi, on the Salmon River, in 1855, and at Franklin, in Cache Valley, in 1860....

"In honorable place in point of seniority [in the settlement of Arizona] are to be noted the Mormon settlements on the Muddy and the Virgin."[7]

Speaking of the quality of their pioneering, F. S. Dellenbaugh, great student of the settlement of the West, wrote:

"It must be acknowledged that the Mormons were wilderness breakers of high quality. They not only broke it, but they kept it broken; and instead of the gin mill and the gambling hall, as cornerstones of their progress and as examples to the natives of the white men's superiority, they planted orchards, gardens, farms, schoolhouses, and peaceful homes."[8]

12 YEARS OF CONFLICT

Even under the best of circumstances pioneering a wilderness is a wearisome, laborious task. In the Great Basin of the West, it was an unending struggle against drought, Indians, difficult travel conditions, poverty, scarcity of water power, excessive freight rates on merchandise brought overland, crickets, grasshoppers, and crop failures. Tragedies were frequent in the fight to secure a foothold in this vast, forbidding country.

One would think that under such conditions there would be little time for spiritual matters. But the Mormons were ever conscious of the reason they had come to this region. It was not for adventure; nor was it to get rich. They had seen more than enough adventure in Missouri and Illinois, and the lands they had left were far richer than those of the valleys of the mountains. They had come to worship God and to build up his work.

Converts from the Nations

It was not uncommon for men suddenly to be called by the Church to go to distant lands as missionaries. Such labor invariably meant great sacrifice on the part of both the missionary and the family at home. While the father preached the gospel, the mother and children did the heavy chores, though they were frequently assisted by members of the priesthood who took time from their own work.

Converts in large numbers gathered to the colonies in the mountains. To assist the poor, the Perpetual Emigrating

Fund Company was formed in 1849, whereby those needing help might borrow money to care for their transportation, the money to be paid back as quickly as possible so that others might be benefited. The fund began functioning in 1850, and within the next thirty years it aided forty thousand people to get to Utah and did a business amounting to $3,600,000.

Before the coming of the railroad, it was impossible to find wagons enough to carry all those who wished to cross the plains. Some of them were so anxious to gather with the Church that they walked, pulling handcarts more than a thousand miles. Most of those who traveled in this way reached the Salt Lake Valley safely and as quickly as those who moved with ox teams.

But bitter tragedy struck two of the handcart companies. The story of these is tersely told in two markers standing in the sage-covered country of Wyoming near South Pass. One of them reads:

"Captain James G. Willie's Handcart Company of Mormon emigrants on their way to Utah, greatly exhausted by the deep snows of an early winter and suffering from lack of food and clothing, had assembled here for reorganization for relief parties from Utah, about the end of October, 1856. Thirteen persons were frozen to death during a single night and were buried here in one grave. Two others died the next day and were buried nearby. Of the company of 404 persons 77 perished before help arrived. The survivors reached Salt Lake City November 9, 1856."

While standing in that lonely, tragic spot one may easily imagine the sorry situation in which these emigrants of 1856 found themselves—a group of hungry men, women, and children huddled together in the midst of a bleak and desolate wilderness, weary from walking more than a thou-

Monument erected in Salt Lake City in honor of the handcart pioneers

sand miles, many of them sick from exhaustion and insufficient food, the handcarts they had pulled standing beside the makeshift tents they had contrived to erect against the swirling snow.

These two companies had been delayed in their departure from Iowa City because their carts were not ready as expected. The authorities in Salt Lake City were not notified of their coming and consequently had made no preparations to see them through. When early storms caught them in the western country of Wyoming, they found themselves in desperate circumstances.

Fortunately, they had been passed on the way by returning missionaries traveling in a light wagon. Sensing the situation, these men pushed on to Salt Lake City with all possible speed. They found the Church in general conference, but when Brigham Young heard their story, he dismissed the meeting and immediately organized teams and wagons to go to the aid of the stricken emigrants. After pushing through harrowing experiences themselves, the rescue party reached the Willie company at Rock Creek Hollow. Leaving aid there, they pressed on to the Martin company some distance further east. The tragic experiences of these two companies were the most sorrowful in the entire movement of the Mormons.

The Lamanites

If the story of the handcart pioneers is a sorrowful chapter in the history of the Mormons, how much more tragic is the story of the Indians in the history of America. The philosophy that the only good Indian was a dead one was all too often the creed of men of the frontier. In marked contrast with this was Brigham Young's policy that "it was manifestly more economical and less expensive to feed and clothe, than to fight them."[1] His generous treatment of the red men led Senator Chase of Ohio to remark that "no governor had ever done so well by the Indians since William Penn."[2]

Respect for the natives arose out of the Book of Mormon. This volume declares that the Indians are descendants of Israel. Their progenitors are known in that volume as the Lamanites, and, in a prophetic vein, the book speaks of a hopeful future for these people.

But though the Mormons were patient and generous, there was occasional trouble. Herds of horses and cattle were a temptation the Indian often could not resist. The natives raided settlements, and two serious outbreaks involved large losses of property. However, in view of the vast territory that they settled, the Mormons had relatively little trouble with the Indians. The history of their relations with the natives demonstrates the wisdom of Brigham Young's policy.

The Utah War

Although the Mormons had little trouble with the Indians, they were to suffer from another source. On July 24, 1857, the inhabitants of Salt Lake City were celebrating both Independence Day and the tenth anniversary of their arrival in the valley. Many of them had gone into one of the mountain canyons adjacent to the city for this purpose.

In the midst of the festivities, a dust-laden and weary horseman hurriedly rode to Brigham Young's tent. He brought ominous news. The United States was sending an army to crush the Mormons! At least that was the story heard from the soldiers, who boasted of what they would do once they reached Salt Lake City.

This had come about largely because two disappointed applicants for government mail contracts had sent to Washington stories that the Mormons were in rebellion against the United States. As was later proved, their stories were absurd. Yet, on only the thin fabric of their tales, the President had ordered twenty-five hundred soldiers to put down a "Mormon rebellion."

Though Brigham Young had properly been installed as governor of the territory, he had been given no notice of the coming of the troops. Not knowing what to expect, the Mormon leaders made preparations. They determined that no other group, armed or otherwise, should again inhabit the homes which they had built. They concluded that if it became necessary they would make Utah the desert it had been before their arrival.

Men were dispatched to do what they could to delay the army and play for time in the hope that something might be done to turn the President from this madness. The prairie was burned and the cattle of the army were stampeded. The bridges which the Mormons had built were destroyed and the fords dredged. But no lives were taken. Because of this carefully executed plan, the army was forced to go into winter quarter in what is now western Wyoming.

But the Mormons were not entirely without friends. Colonel Thomas L. Kane, brother of Elisha Kent Kane, the famed Arctic explorer, had become acquainted with the Saints when they were moving across Iowa and had witnessed the injustices they had suffered. He petitioned the President and received permission to go to Utah to learn the true state of affairs. Largely through his efforts, the President was persuaded to send to Utah a "peace commission" in the spring of 1858.

Brigham Young agreed that the army should be permitted to pass through the city, but should not encamp within it. And lest there should be any violations of this agreement, he put into effect the plan originally decided upon.

When the soldiers entered the valley they found the city desolate and deserted except for a few watchful men armed with flint and steel and sharp axes. The homes and barns were filled with straw ready to be fired in case of violation, and axes were ready to destroy the orchards.

The people had moved to the south, leaving their homes to be burned, as they had done on more than one occasion previously. Some of the army officers and men were deeply affected as they marched through the silent streets, realizing what their coming had meant. Colonel Philip St. George Cooke, who had led the Mormon Battalion on its long march and knew of the wrongs previously inflicted on these

Brigham Young, "the modern Moses"

people, bared his head in reverent respect.

Fortunately there was no difficulty. The army camped forty miles southwest of the city, and the people returned to their homes.

A Man at Work

Joseph Smith had been succeeded by a man as peculiarly fitted in his day to lead the Church as the Prophet had been in his own. Brigham Young, called by some of his biographers "the Modern Moses," had led Israel to another Canaan with its Dead Sea. An interesting description of this man is given by Horace Greeley, editor of the *New York Tribune,* who interviewed the Mormon leader in 1859:

"[Brigham Young] spoke readily,... with no appearance of hesitation or reserve, and with no apparent desire to conceal anything, nor did he repel any of my questions as impertinent. He was very plainly dressed in thin summer clothing, and with no air of sanctimony or fanaticism. In appearance he is a portly, frank, good-natured, rather thickset man of fifty-five, seeming to enjoy life, and to be in no particular hurry to get to heaven. His associates are plain men, evidently born and reared to a life of labor, and looking as little like crafty hypocrites or swindlers as any body of men I ever met."[3]

In 1860 the famed Pony Express was begun. Mail, which first had been carried from the East in slow, ox-drawn wagons, and later on the overland stage, now reached Salt Lake City in six days from St. Joseph, Missouri. The arrival of each pony was an event.

Not long after riders started delivering mail to the valley, news of tremendous significance reached the West. The Southern States had seceded from the Union. America was torn by Civil War. To the Mormons this tragic news was confirmation of the prophecy issued by Joseph Smith

The Pony Express was a significant chapter in America's pioneer history.

on December 25, 1832. Though Utah was not a state, in loyalty she was tied to the Union. That loyalty was expressed by Brigham Young in the first message sent over the overland telegraph in October 1861: "Utah has not seceded, but is firm for the Constitution and laws of our once happy country."[4]

On May 10, 1869, the Union Pacific Railroad building west from the Missouri River, and the Central Pacific, building east from California, met at Promontory, Utah. For the Mormons it meant the end of isolation and ox-team journeys across the plains. It also meant a better understanding of the Saints and their work, as thousands of curious visitors arrived to witness the miracle they had wrought in the desert. The picture that the cross-country traveler saw in these valleys was truly interesting. Here were scores of neat little cities, surrounded by irrigated fields, and beyond these, range lands well stocked with cattle. And on Temple

Completion of the transcontinental railroad at Promontory, Utah, May 10, 1869

The Salt Lake Tabernacle as it appeared soon after construction.

Square in Salt Lake City was a great tabernacle and a partially completed temple.

Ground had been broken for the temple in 1853 and a stone quarry opened in Little Cottonwood Canyon twenty miles south of the city. Hauling the granite, however, posed a serious problem. During the early years of construction, four yoke of oxen required four days to make a round trip in hauling each of the huge foundation stones.

When the army came to Utah, the excavation was filled and the foundation covered to give the site the appearance of a newly plowed field. Construction was not resumed until the policy of the government had been determined.

The work on the temple was executed with great care. Brigham Young, in directing the construction of the temple, had said, "When the Millennium is over...I want that Temple still to stand as a proud monument of the faith, perseverance and industry of the Saints of God in the mountains, in the nineteenth century."[5]

While the temple in Salt Lake City was under construction, similar structures were being built at St. George, 325 miles south; at Manti, 150 miles south; and at Logan, 80 miles north.

In 1863, while work was going forward on the Salt Lake Temple, construction of the Tabernacle on Temple Square was also begun. It has since become one of the most famous buildings in America.

In dimension, the Tabernacle is 250 feet long by 150 feet wide and 80 feet high. The problem of building a roof over this area was serious because neither steel rods, nails, nor bolts were available. First, the forty-four buttresses of sandstone were laid up. These were to become in effect the walls of the building, with doors between. Each of these pillars is twenty feet high, three feet wide, and nine feet through. On these was constructed the huge roof, formed by building a vast bridgework of timbers in lattice fashion. These were pinned together with wooden pegs and bound with rawhide to prevent splitting. This trusswork occupies a space of ten feet from the inside plastered ceiling to the outside roofing. No interior pillar supports the roof.

As a fitting complement to this vast auditorium, Brigham Young requested a magnificent organ. The assignment was given to Joseph Ridges, an organ builder who had joined the Church in Australia. Wood for the organ was hauled by ox team three hundred miles to Salt Lake City from Pine Valley, near St. George, and was laboriously shaped by skilled artisans.

With the completion of the building and the organ in 1870, a choir was organized. This was the beginning of the famed Tabernacle Choir, which has become known throughout the world for its weekly broadcasts from Temple Square and through its concerts in many nations.

The Death of Brigham Young

In 1875 the President of the United States, Ulysses S. Grant, visited Utah. On his arrival in Salt Lake City he was driven through streets thronged with people. He had accepted as true the falsehoods that were still circulated in the East concerning the Mormons, and while passing long lines of rosy-cheeked children who were waving and cheering, he turned to the governor, who was his host, and asked whose children they were. "Mormon children," the governor replied. To this the President remarked, "I have been deceived."[6]

Brigham Young by this time was a man seventy-four years of age. He was in good health, but the trial of the years was telling on him. Life had been a constant struggle from the time he had joined the Church in 1833. In summing up the results of that struggle, he wrote an article for the editor of a New York paper in response to a request for a summary of his labors:

"I thank you for the privilege of representing facts as they are; I will furnish them gladly at any time you make the request.

* * *

"The result of my labors for the past 26 years, briefly summed up, are: The peopling of this Territory by the

127

Latter-day Saints of about 100,000 souls; the founding of over 200 cities, towns and villages inhabited by our people, ...and the establishment of schools, factories, mills and other institutions calculated to improve and benefit our communities.

* * *

"My whole life is devoted to the Almighty's service, and while I regret that my mission is not better understood by the world, the time will come when I will be understood, and I leave to futurity the judgment of my labors and their result as they shall become manifest."[7]

The end of his labors came on August 29, 1877. A few days earlier he had fallen seriously ill. His last words as he lay dying were a call to the man he had succeeded—"Joseph ...Joseph...Joseph...."[8]

13 YEARS OF ENDURANCE

THE history of the Mormon Church is so inextricably interwoven with the doctrine of polygamy that no history of the Church can be complete without some discussion of the practice.

The doctrine was first announced by Joseph Smith at Nauvoo in 1842. Many of the men close to him knew of it and accepted it as a principle of divine pronouncement. However, it was not until 1852 that it was publicly taught. It should be said at the outset that the practice among the Mormons was radically different from that of oriental peoples. Each wife, with her children, occupied a separate house, or, if the wives lived in the same house, as was sometimes the case, in separate quarters. No distinction was made between either of the wives or the children. The husband provided for each family, was responsible for the education of the children, and gave both the children and their mothers the same advantages he would have given to his family under a monogamous relationship. If it was thought he could not do this, he was not permitted to enter into plural marriage.

While the practice was extremely limited—only a small minority of the families were involved—it was the kind of thing of which enemies of the Church could easily take advantage.

Reaction against the doctrine developed throughout the country, and it entered into the presidential campaign

The Presidents of the Church

Joseph Smith
(1830-1844)

Brigham Young
(1847-1877)

John Taylor
(1880-1887)

Wilford Woodruff
(1889-1898)

Lorenzo Snow
(1898-1901)

Joseph F. Smith
(1901-1918)

Heber J. Grant
(1918-1945)

George Albert Smith
(1945-1951)

David O. McKay
(1951-1970)

Joseph Fielding Smith
(1970-1972)

Harold B. Lee
(1972-1973)

Spencer W. Kimball
(1973-1985)

Ezra Taft Benson
(1985-   )

of 1860. When Lincoln was asked what he proposed to do about the Mormons, he replied, "Let them alone."[1] In 1862 Congress passed an anti-polygamy law, but it was aimed at plural marriages and not polygamous relations. Ten years later the Congress passed a bill prohibiting polygamy. It was considered unconstitutional by many people in the nation, and generally by the Mormons. A test case was brought into the courts of Utah and carried through the Supreme Court of the United States, resulting in a decision adverse to the Mormons. In the midst of this difficulty, John Taylor succeeded to the presidency of the Church. The years that followed were truly years of endurance.

"Champion of Liberty"

Elder Taylor was a native of England, where he had been a lay Methodist preacher. He emigrated to Canada about 1832, and heard Mormonism preached for the first time four years later. When he joined the Church, his bold spirit, educated mind, and ready tongue made of him an outstanding advocate of the cause. He served as a missionary in Canada, in his native England, and in France.

This man selected as his motto, "The kingdom of God or nothing."[2] He once remarked: "I do not believe in a religion that cannot have all my affections, but in a religion for which I can both live and die. I would rather have God for my friend than all other influences and powers."[3] In this spirit he defended Mormonism with such vigor that his friends in the Church called him "the Champion of Liberty." He it was who was wounded when Joseph and Hyrum Smith were killed in Carthage jail.

As the senior member of the Council of Twelve Apostles, he succeeded Brigham Young as President of the Church. It was during his administration that the Mormons were again made to feel the bitter hand of persecution. In 1882 the Edmunds Act was passed by Congress, making polygamy punishable by fine or imprisonment—usually imprisonment. No man who had more than one wife could act as a juror in any Utah court. In Idaho, those who were members of the Church were disfranchised. No one who admitted belief in polygamy could become a citizen.

President Taylor foresaw these difficulties. In April, 1882, he counseled the Saints: "Let us treat it [the Edmunds Act] the same as we did this morning in coming through the snow-storm—put up our coat collars...and wait till the storm subsides... There will be a storm in the United States after awhile; and I want our brethren to prepare themselves for it. In the last conference...I advised all who were in debt to take advantage of the prosperous times and pay their debts; so that they might not be in bondage to anyone, and when the storm comes they might be prepared to meet it."[4]

The storm broke in full fury five years later. In 1887 the Edmunds-Tucker Act gave added power to the judges who tried polygamy cases. This act also disincorporated The Church of Jesus Christ of Latter-day Saints, which was ordered by the Supreme Court to wind up its affairs and turn its property over to the nation.

The law was administered with extreme harshness. Thousands of Mormons were disfranchised. A thousand men were imprisoned because they had plural families. Homes were broken. The election machinery was taken from the hands of the people.

Under these conditions John Taylor died on July 25, 1887. He was succeeded by Wilford Woodruff.

A Manifesto to the People

To undertake the responsibility of Church leadership under such circumstances was no small task. Colonies of Latter-day Saints were now scattered from Canada to Mexico. Active missionary work was carried on throughout the United States, in the British Isles, in most of the nations of Europe, and in the islands of the Pacific. In spite of determined opposition, however, many converts to the faith were made in all of these missions. And yet the Church in Utah was dispossessed of its property, and most of its leaders were in prison or were facing prosecution. Under these conditions Wilford Woodruff undertook the responsibility of leadership. He was eighty years of age at the time.

Fortunately, he had been well trained to take up the reins of leadership, having joined the Church only three years after its organization. He had marched from Ohio to Missouri to aid his brethren when they were driven from Jackson County, and he had passed through the Missouri persecutions. As we have previously seen, he was a powerful missionary in England, where he had brought more than two thousand converts into the Church.

He had gone west as one of the pioneer company, and Brigham Young was in his wagon when he made the prophetic statement concerning the Salt Lake Valley, "This is the right place." He had participated in most of the significant events connected with the building of the territory since that time.

But now, most progress had ceased under the heavy hand of law enforcement, and President Woodruff was responsible for finding a way out of the difficulty. As he struggled with the problem, he turned to the scriptures for direction.

In a revelation given to the Church in 1841, the Prophet

Joseph Smith had declared as the word of the Lord, "Verily, verily, I say unto you, that when I give a commandment to any of the sons of men to do a work unto my name, and those sons of men go with all their might and with all they have to perform that work, and cease not their diligence, and their enemies come upon them and hinder them from performing that work, behold it behooveth me to require that work no more at the hands of those sons of men, but to accept of their offerings."[5] Another fundamental teaching of the Church which also applied is the twelfth article of faith of the organization. It reads, "We believe in being subject to kings, presidents, rulers, and magistrates, in obeying, honoring, and sustaining the law."

What was to be done under the circumstances? The practice had come by revelation.

And it came to an end by the same means. After earnest prayer before the Lord, President Woodruff issued on October 6, 1890, what is known in Church history as the "Manifesto." It declared an end to the practice of plural marriage. Since that time the Church has neither practiced nor sanctioned such marriages.

The End of an Era

On April 6, 1893, the great temple in Salt Lake City was declared completed, and the building was dedicated to God as his holy house. Prior to its dedication, nonmembers of the Church were invited to go through the building, and its various facilities were explained to them. Since its dedication, only members of the Church in good standing have been permitted to enter.

It was fitting that Wilford Woodruff should have lived to offer the dedicatory prayer. Forty-six years earlier he had driven the stake to mark the location of the building. For forty years he had watched its construction. Its dedication

The Salt Lake Temple nearing completion of construction

was one of the great events in the history of the area.

Before his death in September 1898, President Woodruff was to participate in another significant event. Although the residents of the territory had applied for statehood in 1849, this boon had been denied because of anti-Mormon agitation throughout the nation. But on January 4, 1896, Utah was admitted to the Union as a state. In ceremonies incident to the occasion, President Woodruff was asked to offer the prayer. The prayer is indicative of the man's vision:

"Almighty God, the Creator of heaven and earth, thou who are the God of nations and the Father of the spirits of all men, we humbly bow before Thee on this great occasion. . . .

"When we gaze upon these fertile valleys with their abundant products of fields and garden, . . . their pleasant homes and prosperous inhabitants . . . and contrast these with the barren and silent wastes which greeted the eyes of the pioneers when first they looked upon these dry sage lands less than half a century ago, our souls are filled with wonder and with praise! . . .

"And now, when the efforts of several decades to secure the priceless boon of perfect political liberty . . . have at length been crowned with glorious success, we feel that to thee, our father and our God, we are indebted for this inestimable blessing. . . .

"We pray Thee to bless the president of the United States and his cabinet, that they may be inspired to conduct the affairs of this great nation in wisdom, justice and equity, that its rights may be maintained at home and abroad and that all its citizens may enjoy the privileges of free men. . . . And may the privileges of free government be extended to every land and clime, until tyranny and oppression shall be broken down to rise no more, until all nations shall unite for the common good, that war may cease, that the voice of strife may be hushed, that universal brotherhood may prevail, and Thou, O God, shall be honored everywhere as the Everlasting Father and the King of peace!"[6]

14

THE SUNSHINE OF GOOD WILL

PRESIDENT Wilford Woodruff died September 2, 1898, and at the age of 84, when most men have laid aside their life's work, Lorenzo Snow succeeded him as President of the Church. As with the men who had gone before him, early in life he had gained extensive experience in the Church, serving on missions both at home and abroad.

When he took over the leadership of the organization, the Church was in a desperate financial condition. The nation had passed through a severe economic depression, which had been felt in the West as elsewhere. Then, too, under the anti-polygamy prosecution, the payment of tithing had seriously decreased. The property of the Church had been confiscated, and much of the incentive for paying tithing had gone. The organization was under a staggering burden of debt.

Under these conditions, President Snow made a trip in the spring of 1899 to the town of St. George in southern Utah. Drought had blighted the land. The preceding winter had been the driest in thirty-five years, and the one preceding that the driest in thirty-four years. The people were discouraged, for it appeared as if a curse had come over what once had been a garden-land.

By inspiration, as President Snow said, he spoke to the assembled Saints on the law of tithing. Had not the Lord said through the prophet Malachi that Israel had robbed Him in tithes and offerings? And had He not also given them a promise that if they would bring their tithes into the storehouse He would open the windows of heaven and pour out a blessing that they would not have room enough to receive it?

The President then went on to promise the Saints that if they would faithfully pay their tithes, they could plant their crops and rain would come. The people heeded the counsel. They paid their tithes, not only in St. George, but

The St. George Temple

throughout the Church as the President continued his appeals for obedience to this commandment of God. But weeks passed in the southern colony, and still the hot winds blew and the crops wilted.

Then one morning in August a telegram was laid on the President's desk: "Rain in St. George." The creeks and rivers filled, and the crops matured.

In 1907 the last of the Church's debt was paid. Since then, the Church has been free of financial stress.

Joseph F. Smith

Lorenzo Snow died October 10, 1901. He was succeeded by Joseph F. Smith, son of Hyrum Smith, who was murdered in Carthage jail. His life reflects the history of Mormonism from a position of ignominy to one of wide respect.

He was born November 13, 1838, at Far West, Missouri. At the time, his father was a prisoner of the mob-militia, whose avowed purpose was to exterminate the Mormons. When he was an infant, his mother carried him in the flight from Far West to Illinois.

One of his earliest recollections was of that historic night of June 27, 1844, when he was five years of age. A knock was heard on his mother's window, and a trembling voice whispered that his father had been killed by the Carthage mob. As a seven-year-old boy he heard the roar of guns incident to the final expulsion of the Mormons from Nauvoo, and before reaching his eighth birthday he drove a team of oxen most of the way across Iowa.

In 1848 the family crossed the plains. It was no small task for a ten-year-old boy to yoke and unyoke oxen as well as drive most of the day. When the boy was thirteen, his mother died, her vitality exhausted by the experiences through which she had passed.

Two years later he was called on a mission to the Hawaiian Islands. Making his way to the Coast, he worked in a shingle mill to earn money to pay his way to the Islands.

Following his missionary experience in Hawaii, he served the Church in the British Isles as well as in other fields of labor. He became President of the Church in 1901.

Shortly after this, Reed Smoot, a member of the Council of the Twelve Apostles, was elected U.S. Senator from Utah. His seat was soon contested by political enemies who played on the old polygamy issue. It was Joseph F. Smith, however, rather than the senator, who became the principal target of attack. He was cartooned and slandered throughout the nation. But he had seen so much of intolerance that he passed over this new outburst, saying, "There are those...who will shut their eyes to every virtue and to every good thing connected with this latter day work, and will pour out floods of falsehood and misrepresentation against the people of God. I forgive them for this. I leave them in the hand of the just Judge."[1]

In spite of all such attacks, these were years of progress for the Church. Missionary work was extended. Scores of beautiful buildings were erected, including three temples— one in Arizona, one in Canada, and one in the Hawaiian Islands. A bureau of information was established on Temple Square in Salt Lake City to greet the thousands of tourists who came from all parts of the world, usually out of curiosity. They learned the facts concerning the Mormons, and the old hatred, the old bitterness slowly gave way.

On November 19, 1918, Joseph F. Smith died. Newspapers which had slandered his character paid editorial homage to him, and prominent men throughout the nation voiced high tribute to his memory. The years had vindicated him and the cause to which he had dedicated his life.

The LDS temple in Washington, D.C.

Heber J. Grant

Four days following the death of President Smith, Heber J. Grant became President of the Church. His father, who had been a counselor to Brigham Young, had died when the boy was nine days old. He was born November 22, 1856, the first of the presidents of the Church to have been born in the West.

Heber J. Grant was by nature a practical man. He had a recognized talent in the field of finance, and as a young man he made an enviable record in business. But at the same time he was active in Church affairs, and when only twenty-six years of age, he was ordained a member of the Council of the Twelve Apostles. From that time forward he

142

was a zealous worker in the cause of Mormonism.

His financial abilities were shown to marked degree when, during the depression of the Nineties, he was sent east by the President of the Church to borrow money. In spite of business conditions and the popular attitude toward the Mormons, he returned with hundreds of thousands of dollars, which proved a great boon in those difficult times.

Heber J. Grant was also a leading figure in the establishment of the western beet sugar industry. The Church was interested in this because it meant a cash crop for

The LDS Church Administration Building in Salt Lake City, Utah

thousands of its members. Accordingly, he materially assisted in the founding of this industry, which has put millions of dollars into the hands of western farmers.

One of President Grant's favorite projects was giving away books. The funds for this purpose he called his "cigarette money" because, he claimed, the money some of his friends wasted on cigarettes he was able to spend on books. During his lifetime he passed out more than a hundred thousand volumes at his own expense.

Unflinching in his loyalty to his church and its teachings, he was nevertheless a great friend maker. Leaders in business, education, and government were his intimate friends, and his capacity for getting along with people greatly helped in breaking down the wall of prejudice against the Mormons.

His administration was an era of progress. The Church passed its hundredth anniversary in 1930, commemorating the event with a great celebration. Unhampered by the oppression of religious bigots, freed from the brutality of mobs, strong enough to assert its power for good, it flourished in an era of good will previously unknown in all of its history.

George Albert Smith

President Grant died May 14, 1945, in his eighty-ninth year. He was succeeded by George Albert Smith. President Smith was born April 4, 1870. As a young man he served a mission in the southern states, and, after becoming a member of the Council of the Twelve Apostles, he presided over the affairs of the Church in Europe.

One of his major interests was Scouting. He served as a member of the National Executive Board of Boy Scouts of America and received the highest awards for local and national service to the cause of Scouting. An official citation given him by national officials stated that "to his enthusiasm for its [Scouting's] program must be largely traced the fact that Utah stands above all other states in the percentage of boys who are Scouts."[2]

For many years President Smith took a leading part in preserving the story of America's pioneers. He was the organizer and served as president of the Utah Pioneer Trails and Landmarks Association, under whose sponsorship the Mormon trail from Nauvoo to Salt Lake City was marked with stone and bronze. He likewise served as vice-president of the Oregon Trail Memorial Association, and was one of the organizers of the American Pioneer Trails Association.

David O. McKay

President Smith passed away on April 4, 1951, his eighty-first birthday. His funeral was held in the Salt Lake Tabernacle on April 7, and two days later, in the same building, members of the Church, "in solemn assembly," sustained David Oman McKay as president of the Church. President McKay was then seventy-seven, having been born at Huntsville, Utah, September 8, 1873.

By training he was an educator, but he devoted most of his life to the Church. He was named a member of the Council of the Twelve Apostles at the age of 32. A man of commanding appearance and dynamic personality, he won friends for the Church wherever he went on his worldwide travels in the interest of the cause to which he had given his heart.

He promoted a greatly expanded building program which created thousands of new houses of worship; temples in Switzerland, England, New Zealand, and the United States; and a dramatic expansion of the Church school system.

Joseph Fielding Smith

President McKay passed away in Salt Lake City, Janu-

The New Zealand Temple

ary 18, 1970, at the age of 96, and was succeeded five days later by Joseph Fielding Smith, President of the Council of the Twelve Apostles, of which he had been a member for sixty years. He was the son of Joseph F. Smith, the sixth president of the Church, and a grandson of Hyrum Smith, who was murdered with the Prophet Joseph in 1844.

President Joseph Fielding Smith was a lifelong student of the doctrine and history of the Church. His extensive writings on these subjects made of him a recognized authority in these fields, and for many years he served as Church Historian and Recorder, responsible for maintaining the extensive archives which have become a treasure house of information, not only on the Church and its history, but also on the cultures in which it has developed.

Harold B. Lee

President Smith died in Salt Lake City on July 2, 1972, and was succeeded by Harold B. Lee on July 7th of the same year. In 1936, when the nation and most of the world were paralyzed by a tragic economic depression, officers of the Church, building on principles laid down by Joseph Smith, inaugurated what was termed the Church Security Program, later called the Church Welfare Program. Governments were trying to stem the tide of unemployment with various make-work and dole systems. But the Church taught the principle that in times of stress, responsibility for remedying the problem lay first with the individual, then with his family, and then with the Church, rather than with his government. Elder Lee was given the major task for setting up a system under which "the curse of idleness would be done away with, the evils of a dole abolished, and independence, industry, thrift and self respect be once more established amongst our people."[3] All Church members were expected to work together to help those in distress.

Farms were acquired; processing, production, and distribution facilities were constructed; and other resources were put in motion to provide the unemployed with the opportunity to fulfill their needs and preserve their integrity. This program, which continues to expand as the Church grows, has been commended by social welfare experts from many parts of the world.

Spencer W. Kimball

President Lee died in Salt Lake City, December 26, 1973. Four days later Spencer W. Kimball was given the reins of presidency. Church membership had now passed the three-million mark, and within five years under his dynamic leadership another million members were added to the rolls.

Spencer W. Kimball was born in Salt Lake City, March 28, 1895, but was reared in Arizona. There he served in many Church capacities while carrying on his private business. He was ordained an Apostle in 1943 and traveled over much of the earth building and strengthening the kingdom.

Although small of stature, he was a veritable dynamo in fulfilling the responsibilities of president of an expanding Church. He repeatedly called on the membership to "lengthen our stride" and "quicken our pace." New missions were opened in many parts of the earth, and thousands of young men and women served in those missions, giving freely of their time and means to teach the restored gospel of Jesus Christ to the nations of the earth.

Of great significance was President Kimball's announcement of June 9, 1978, that the Lord "has heard our prayers, and by revelation has confirmed that the long-promised day has come when every faithful, worthy

The LDS Church Office Building in Salt Lake City, Utah

man in the Church may receive the holy priesthood, with power to exercise its divine authority, and enjoy with his loved ones every blessing that flows therefrom, including the blessing of the temple. Accordingly, all worthy male members of the Church may be ordained to the priesthood without regard for race or color."[4] News of this change in a policy that had been observed for almost a century and a half was carried in the media across the world, and the response was highly favorable.

During the years of President Kimball's leadership, the Church received a growing measure of respect. Three items indicative of this may be mentioned:

As we have previously noted, the Latter-day Saints were driven from Missouri by an inhumane and illegal extermination order issued by Governor Boggs. On June 25, 1976, his successor in office several times removed, Governor Christopher S. Bond, issued another executive order which reads in part: "Whereas, Governor Boggs' order clearly contravened the rights to life, liberty, property and religious freedom as guaranteed by the Constitution of the United States, as well as the Constitution of the State of Missouri; . . .

"Now, therefore, I . . . do hereby order as follows: Expressing on behalf of all Missourians our deep regret for the injustice and undue suffering which was caused by this 1838 order, I hereby rescind Executive Order Number 44 dated October 27, 1838, issued by Governor Lilburn W. Boggs."[5]

In 1978, an impressive memorial to the women of the Church was dedicated in Nauvoo, Illinois. It portrays in a variety of bronze figures set in a spacious park women young and older, mothers and children who lived in Nauvoo and were compelled to leave their homes and flee to the sanctuary they established in the mountains, many of them dying on the way. On the occasion of this dedication, national and state officials and men and women of prominence from Illinois and other parts of the nation paid tribute to the Mormons who once had built a beautiful city from the swamplands they found there.

Also in 1978, the President of the United States signed a bill passed by Congress which repealed the Edmunds-Tucker Act of 1887—the legislation that had been employed to disincorporate the Church and escheat its property in the harsh persecutions and prosecutions against the Latter-day Saints during the last decades of the nineteenth century.

Ezra Taft Benson

President Spencer W. Kimball passed away November 5, 1985, and five days later, on November 10, Ezra Taft Benson was set apart as the thirteenth president of the Church. Upon becoming Church president he led six million members located in countries throughout the world.

Named after his great-grandfather, who was a member of the Quorum of the Twelve Apostles, Ezra Taft Benson was born in Whitney, Idaho, in 1899. While still in his teens he shouldered a large portion of the responsibilities of operating a farm while his father served a full-time mission for the Church. Upon reaching maturity, he was called on a mission to Great Britain, and after returning graduated with honors from Brigham Young University. Following the completion of his master's degree at Iowa State University, he served as a county agricultural agent and then as an extension economist in Boise, Idaho. In 1938 he went to

151

Washington, D.C., as Executive Secretary of the National Council of Farmer Cooperatives. There he was named stake president, a position he had previously held in Idaho. In 1943, he was sustained a member of the Church's Council of the Twelve Apostles. When Dwight David Eisenhower was elected United States President in 1952, he asked Elder Benson to become Secretary of Agriculture in his administration. Elder Benson accepted and served with distinction in the President's cabinet for eight years.

Almost immediately after his call as the Church's prophet, President Benson emphasized to Church members the reading and use of the Book of Mormon. "We not only need to *say* more about the Book of Mormon, but we need to *do* more with it," he declared.[6] Since that time the use of this volume of scripture in missionary work and in personal and family studies and teaching has increased dramatically.

In their first Christmas message, the new First Presidency made an eloquent appeal for the disaffected, the critical, and the transgressors to "come back. Come back and feast at the table of the Lord, and taste again the sweet and satisfying fruits of fellowship with the Saints."[7] President Benson has also spoken out strongly in support of family strength and solidarity.

President Benson presides over the Church in a new era, an era of widespread respect and admiration and ever-accelerating growth. But the present also has its challenges as the work moves over the world. The Church is no longer a Utah church or an American church. Not alone in the United States and Canada is the work strong and growing; in other areas of the world the rate of growth is even greater. In the British Isles and Western

Europe, throughout Mexico and Central and South America, in Africa, in the ancient lands of Asia, in Australia, in New Zealand, and in the islands of the South Pacific are found strong and developing congregations of the Saints. Once converts in the overseas missions "gathered to Zion." Now they remain in their native lands to build Zion there with the identical organization, the identical programs, and the same teachings found wherever the Church has been established.

Today the same testimony Joseph Smith first bore to his neighbors in upper-state New York may be heard in a score of languages, declaring that God lives, that Jesus is the Christ, that His ancient gospel has been restored to the earth, and that the Church of Jesus Christ is again available to all mankind.

NOTES

Chapter 1

1. In Preston Nibley, *Joseph Smith, the Prophet* (Salt Lake City: Deseret News Press, 1946), pp. 21–22.

2. Joseph Smith-History 1:11–19 (formerly Joseph Smith 2:11–19).

3. Joseph Smith-History 1:24–25.

Chapter 2

1. Joseph Smith-History 1:28–50.

2. Oliver Cowdery's account of the experience as found in a letter from Cowdery to W. W. Phelps dated 28 May 1835. (See *Cowdery's Letters on the Bringing in of the New Dispensation* [Burlington, Wis.: Free Press Print, 1899], pp. 26–27.) The letter was first published in 1854.

3. Joseph Smith-History 1:54, 59.

4. Joseph Smith-History 1:65.

5. John 10:16.

Chapter 3

1. See D&C 13.

2. See Matthew 3:13–15.

3. See D&C 128:20.

4. 2 Nephi 27:12.

5. In Joseph Smith, *History of The Church of Jesus Christ of Latter-day Saints,* 7 vols., 2nd ed. rev., edited by B. H. Roberts (Salt Lake City: The Church of Jesus Christ of Latter-day Saints, 1932–51), 1:55. Hereafter cited as HC.

6. Moroni 10:5.

Chapter 4

1. D&C 21:1.

2. In B. H. Roberts, *A Comprehensive History of The Church of Jesus Christ of Latter-day Saints, Century One,* 6 vols. (Salt Lake City: The Church of Jesus Christ of Latter-day Saints, 1930), 2:470. Hereafter cited as CHC.

3. *Autobiography of Parley P. Pratt,* ed. Parley P. Pratt, Jr. (Salt Lake City: Deseret Book, 1938), p. 48.

4. *Autobiography of Parley P. Pratt,* p. 52.

5. CHC 1:255.

Chapter 5

1. D&C 76:22–24.

2. John 14:2.

3. 1 Corinthians 15:40–42.

4. D&C 87:2–3.

5. D&C 88:118.

6. D&C 93:36.

7. D&C 130:18–19.

8. In Lucy Mack Smith, *History of Joseph Smith,* ed. Preston Nibley, reprint (Salt Lake City: Bookcraft, 1954), p. 230.

9. *History of Joseph Smith,* pp. 231–32.

10. "Kirtland Temple (Mormon)," *Architecture Forum* 64 (March 1936): 179.

11. D&C 110:1–4.

Chapter 6

1. CHC 1:311–12.

2. See HC 1:372.

3. See HC 1:374.

4. D&C 119.

5. HC 3:157.

6. HC 3:175.

7. HC 3:190–91.

Chapter 7

1. HC 3:375.

2. In Matthias F. Cowley, *Wilford Woodruff* (Salt Lake City: Bookcraft, 1964), pp. 104–5.

3. CHC 2:45.

4. HC 4:457.

5. HC 4:80.

6. John 3:5.

7. 1 Corinthians 15:29.

8. In George Q. Cannon, *Life of Joseph Smith the Prophet* (Salt Lake City: Deseret Book, 1964), pp. 354–55.

9. *The Mormons* (Philadelphia: King and Baird, 1850), pp. 3–4.

10. In Cannon, *Life of Joseph Smith the Prophet*, p. 353.

11. *Figures of the Past from the Leaves of Old Journals* (Boston: Roberts Brothers, 1883), p. 376.

Chapter 8

1. Dallin H. Oaks, "The Suppression of the *Nauvoo Expositor*," *Utah Law Review* 9(1965): 875.

2. HC 6:448.

3. *Utah Law Review* 9(1965):903.

4. HC 6:537.

5. HC 6:540.

6. HC 6:546.

7. HC 6:549–50.

8. HC 6:554.

9. D&C 135:4.

10. See HC 6:570.

11. HC 6:605.

12. See HC 6:612–21.

13. HC 5:85.

Chapter 9

1. In Edward W. Tullidge, *The Women of Mormondom* (New York: Tullidge and Crandall, 1877), pp. 307–8.

2. CHC 3:52.

3. Journal History, 13 and 18 July 1846.

4. CHC 3:119–20.

5. *The Mormons,* pp. 9–10.

Chapter 10

1. D&C 136:1–4, 19–21, 23–30.

2. *Millenial Star* 12(15 Mar. 1850):82–83.

3. *Millenial Star* 12(15 Mar. 1850):146.

Chapter 11

1. See Journal History, 25 July 1847.

2. Diary of Wilford Woodruff, 28 July 1847.

3. CHC 3:319.

4. CHC 3:362.

5. In Preston Nibley, *Brigham Young: the Man and His Work* (Salt Lake City: Deseret News Press, 1936), pp. 127–28.

6. CHC 3:349–50.

7. *Mormon Settlement in Arizona* (Phoenix: James H. McClintock, 1921), pp. 4–6.

8. Ibid., p. 6.

Chapter 12

1. CHC 4:51.

2. *History of Brigham Young 1847–1867* (Berkeley, Cal.: MassCal Associates, 1964), pp. 159–60.

3. *An Overland Journey* (New York: Alfred A. Knopf, 1963), pp. 183–84.

4. *Deseret News,* 23 Oct. 1861, p. 189.

5. *Journal of Discourses,* 26 vols. (London: Latter-day Saints' Book Depot, 1854–86), 10:254.

6. CHC 5:504–5.

7. In Preston Nibley, *Brigham Young: the Man and His Work,* p. 492.

8. See Susa Young Gates and Leah D. Widtsoe, *The Life Story of Brigham Young* (New York: the Macmillan Company, 1930), p. 362.

Chapter 13

1. CHC 5:70.

2. See *Journal of Discourses* 6:18–27. The phrase was first used by Brigham Young in a letter to a Colonel Alexander, dated 16 October 1857. The text of the letter can be found in *The Millenial Star* 20 (30 Jan. 1858): 75–76.

3. In B. H. Roberts, *The Life of John Taylor* (Salt Lake City: George Q. Cannon and Sons, 1892), p. 423.

4. Ibid., pp. 360–61.

5. D&C 124:49.

6. *The Salt Lake Herald,* 7 Jan. 1896, p. 1.

Chapter 14

1. In Joseph Fielding Smith, *Life of Joseph F. Smith,* 2nd ed. (Salt Lake City: Deseret Book, 1969), p. 351.

2. In Preston Nibley, *The Presidents of the Church* (Salt Lake City: Deseret Book, 1941), p. 366.

3. Message of the First Presidency, in Conference Report, Oct. 1936, p. 3.

4. In *Ensign,* July 1978, p. 75.

5. Executive order of 25 June 1976, copy in Archives of The Church of Jesus Christ of Latter-day Saints.

6. In Conference Report, April 1986, p. 4; or in *Ensign,* May 1986, p. 5.

7. In *Church News,* 22 Dec. 1985, p. 3.